Lizzie Scott says "I have been happily married for over 30 years and have four kids who somehow think they are adults... but I know I'm not old enough to be the parent of an adult, but I also know I was there at the births... says a lot about me does that :-)

All my adult life has been dedicated to the welfare of children and ensuring they get the best service possible from me, my family and the professional groups that are supposed to represent them. I hope between all the adults we did a good job, but at the same time just know some kids got sold short by the system.

I adore my family. My husband, kids and grandchildren are the most important thing in life to me."

Lizzie Scott hopes her stories will be educational to some, a comfort to others who are travelling an uncertain path with a child who has deep emotional and physical wounds and, an inspiration to those who are considering entering the field of childcare as either a foster carer or a social worker.

Lizzie Scott was a foster carer for over 24 years, during which time she and her family shared their home with more than 200 children, of all ages and backgrounds. The true-life stories which she will share show the suffering and courage of some of the most vulnerable children in our society and of the dedicated work foster carers, social workers and outside agencies give to enable them to move on to better futures, whether that is through a return to their birth families, or on to new families via adoption, or long term care.

Lizzie says "Our family went into fostering when our youngest child started playschool" as it was then known. "The idea was that we would foster for a few years so that I didn't miss out on all the school activities that young children want their parents to attend." Once our children became more independent I would get a 'proper' job.

But of course, fostering quickly becomes a way of life for many who choose to 'work' in this part of the caring sector.

Nowadays there can be big rewards for those who work in the fostering field of childcare but...the biggest reward any foster carer can ever receive is that first smile from a 'frozen, unemotional and unresponsive' child, and that first truly relaxed and happy hug freely given and warmly received from the child to the carer.

Much consideration is given to matching the race and religious background of a child entering the care system. Perhaps there would be less fostering breakdowns if more thought was put into matching the social worker and the foster carer as a foster carer will always go that extra mile for a social worker they like and trust.

Lizzie says "I would like to give special acknowledgement to some of the excellent social workers that shared in the traumas, tears, tantrums and happiness that our family and the children that shared our lives went through."

Visit the author's website at www.lizziescottbooks.com

Follow Lizzie Scott on Facebook for all the latest news.

Lizzie Scott has asserted her right to be identified as the author of this Work in accordance with the Copyright, Designs and Patents Act 1988

All rights reserved.

No part of this publication may be reproduced, stored in a retrieval system, or transmitted, in any form or by any means, electronic, mechanical, photocopying, recording or otherwise, without the prior permission in writing of the copyright owner, nor be otherwise circulated in any form of binding or cover other than that in which it is published and without a similar condition including this condition.

This book is dedicated to my
Mum and dad
Thank you for being the
wonderful parents you are.
Without the love and guidance which you
freely gave throughout my childhood and
adult life, I wouldn't be the person that I am today
I love you

They're at the door

They're at the door
and so unsure
of what they'll find inside.
And you are there
with all your care
later, admit you cried

Now they're here
slowly vanishes their fear
a reaction to love and care.
But soon they'll go
to where? Don't know
but we hope they'll be happy there

The day you fear
is finally here
and you stand smiling to wave goodbye.
God Bless my dears
your future years
now I'll go inside and cry.

But the phone soon rings
and social sings
"We've another child for you".
You dry your eye
heave a sigh
plenty more work to do.

Chapter 1

The bitter cold snow; fog; sleet and bone chilling winds of December had continued into the New Year. It looked like we were in for a few more weeks of freezing rain, snow and sleet here in Britain before we could look forward to discarding the winter woollies for some brighter, warmer, sunnier weather clothes.

As someone who really dislikes the cold wintery weather I eagerly awaited for spring to arrive, then summer to awaken, when the children could happily play outside without fear of catching colds and we could enjoy days in the park without getting covered in mud.

The children, unlike most adults, of course were just loving having fun in the seasonal chill and being able to play in the snow, though were not so keen on the rainy days, when they were forced to play indoors. They had been able to build snowmen when the snow had blown in and of course, puddles were something to be splashed through and not avoided, even in their new school shoes!

One of the many things about children that has always amazed me is their ability to play outside no matter how cold it becomes or how wet they were…it is the adults who spoil their fun by making them play inside when raining, yet we will allow them to merrily dance through a snow storm with squeals of delight.

Children do and have always fascinated me and I often wish our minds could take us back sometimes to when we were young and discovering things for the first time, wondering what things were and how they work. Sometimes I would lie on the floor and try to imagine being tiny and seeing things for the first time. It's interesting to get down low and look around at what a child can see. It's not much compared to adults so I suppose that's why, as they grow a little taller and can see what is on a chair, table or unit and curiosity sets in all sorts of discovery and adventures start for them. What a wonderful world safe, secure and cherished children must live in.

David, who had been home for Christmas was now settled back at university after the Christmas holidays and Edward, James and Claire were settled back at their respective schools having fun catching up with all their friends holiday news. We had also been enjoying a rare few weeks of having no 'borrowed' children in our home, enabling me to spend time alone while our children were at school to catch up with my friends and, when the children were home to spend special family time with them. Weekends were lovely and a hub of family activity, though rather chilly for going out.

Our last placement, which was one of several that had been fairly short lasting and, to be honest, mostly not like working at all since our experience with Jenny and Chloe[*], had ended shortly before the children had broken up for the Christmas holidays. I had the distinct impression that the Department of Social Services (or at least some of the very good social workers we worked with who knew us well) was trying to look after us after the trauma of those little girls and had deliberately given us placements that, though taxing at times, were in no way as emotionally wearing on our whole family.

We had been looking after twin five year old boys, who came to stay with our family for a few weeks while their mother had been in hospital.

We had agreed to a respite placement because, unfortunately, there was no extended family living locally to look after them, and the extended family that lived some miles away had commitments with Christmas fast approaching and their own families to care for which made it impossible for them to be able to cater to the needs of these two little boys.

It's always very sad when a parent has to go to hospital and all their extended family live many miles from them. On top of any concerns the parent may have about impending operations, the worry about their children must be huge, especially if they have never had social services involved in their lives before.

---

[*] Tormented by Lizzy Scott

Some parents must be scared by horror stories periodically found in the media, that they will not have their children returned to them, or that the foster carers will not be very nice people and will treat their children differently to how they are used to within their own family unit.

This isn't just a problem faced by single parents either. Many two parent families have to rely on fostering placements at times like this because one parent has to go to work and just cannot get the time off to look after their children for what could potentially be a long period of time.

With respite placements it is very important to work closely with the birth parents in order to reassure them that their children will be well cared for and, where possible, the foster carer should take guidance from the birth parents regarding routines and discipline.

The best thing about planned respite placements is that the foster carer and the birth parents can sometimes spend time, even if this is only limited due to other commitments, to get to know each other and for the birth parents to share as much information as possible about their children's likes and dislikes as well as their daily routine. It also means the children can have visits to the foster home and see where they will eat, sleep and play as well as meet who they will be sharing their time with. And a bonus for the foster carer is they can observe the children alone as well as with any 'home grown' children to assess for any potential peer relationship difficulties.

Connor and Riley's mother unfortunately had more concerns than most mums I had met through fostering. Both Connor and Riley had been born with heart problems. They also suffered from really bad eczema and were asthmatic.

Howard and I also had concerns about caring for the boys and we were extremely grateful for the time that we were allowed to spend with their mum, getting reassurance from her that she had confidence in us, as we reassured her that we would look after her children as though they were our own.

Connor and Riley's mother explained the boys skin care routine and told us how important it was that we deviated as little as possible from it. They both had to be moisturized all over twice a day, once after their morning wash and again after their evening bath. We were to use no scented children's bubble bath as these could cause a flare up which would result in them scratching their little bodies so much that their skin would bleed.

It was important also, their mother explained, to keep the children as settled and calm as possible not only for the sake of their hearts, but because if they became distressed they could have an eczema outbreak as well as an asthma attack. I think the asthma was my biggest concern at that time as we had never cared for an asthmatic child before, but knew the implications could be extremely serious, as our friend Elizabeth's daughter was asthmatic. We were concerned the problems could be even more serious with the children's heart complaint.

I took copious notes when spending time with their mum, and played on the floor with the boys and toys when they came for visits to get used to us as a family, which would hopefully make their stay with us seem more like a little holiday, than any sort of punishment because their mum was going into hospital.

One of the things that is very important with all fostering placements, is to reassure the children that they are not with you because they have done something wrong, as many children seem to believe that they are the reason they have had to leave their family. This has to be done in a way that doesn't run their birth parents down as most children, no matter how dysfunctional their background may be, love their parents and want, initially, to be returned to them. It is only after spending time in a non-abusive and safe environment that some children come to understand how sad and possibly bad their previous life had been. Fortunately, this respite placement was not to continue to a long term pre-adoption one and the children would be going home again.

We were so lucky to have spent time with this little family prior to them sharing our home as, when the day finally came that they went to school from their mum's home and were collected from school by their social worker and brought to our home, they came with smiles and not fear of the unknown.

Connor and Riley were absolutely adorable children with a ready smile for the world and were just so very, very friendly, happy and responsive children. With their happy disposition it was a shame to see them suffer so badly with their eczema, which was literally all over them even with the twice daily dousing with special creams and lotions. They also had to use their inhalers and puffers several times a day to help prevent them having asthma attacks.

Fortunately, during the time they stayed with us there were no bad asthma attacks, but the eczema just didn't calm down at all no matter how calm our home life seemed to be.

For their age Connor and Riley were very well aware of their routine regarding the medicines and moisturizing and would come to remind me if they thought I had forgotten because I was a little slower than their mum in getting everything organized, which was great as it felt like I had my own little mobile alarm clocks keeping me on track.

One job Howard has always enjoyed since becoming a dad is the bedtime routine. He hasn't always been home for the water fun in the bath part of it, but has always been there to read the bedtime story and enjoys using different voices for the many different charactors in each book he reads. One particular favourite is The Faraway Tree - not only favourite for Howard but also for the children he has read it to over the years. Fortunately Connor and Riley were just the right age for him to be reading them this book and the excitement on their little faces at bedtime was a joy to see.

Connor and Riley stayed with our family for three weeks and, to be honest, that time shot past so quickly because they didn't seem like 'working' weeks. Their mum kept in touch with telephone calls and we went to visit a couple of times while she was in hospital, but she didn't want her children seeing her while she looked poorly so these visits were limited to only one a week and the time we stayed limited to a maximum of thirty minutes, which seemed to suit the children as well because being young, all they really wanted to do once they had cuddled their mum was get home to play with Edward, James and Claire.

For Connor, Riley and our family the last few days of the placement had been a mixture of joy and sorrow. Obviously everyone was overjoyed that their mum was recovering well enough for her to be able to go home and care for her children, especially with Christmas just around the corner and we had some hope that this year we would manage to have a Christmas with just our children at home, a rare occurrence in the years since we had been looking after children for the local authority…and sorrow that we would be saying goodbye to such lovely little boys, who came to our home without the usual sadness that normally accompanied the children that shared our family life.

Chapter 2

Of course, time out is quite a rare commodity when you are a fostering family, so we all knew it was only a matter of time before we would have that telephone call asking us to take in another child or a little family. We had established ourselves over the past six years as a family that preferred to keep siblings together as we knew we wouldn't want our children to be placed with different families, if we had ever needed the support we offered families through fostering.

Our first placement of this year was a little different to usual. For a start, the family actually lived very close to us, only a couple of streets away, where we usually had children from a neighbouring town or village. I was told by social services that the father would be bringing the children to our home alone the following evening and the mother would be given my phone number and address so we could arrange contact between us. I was also told that I would be taking the children to visit the mother in her home (what had been their home) before she came to our home to visit them.

This in itself was very strange, as it is important that the children settle into their new environment and, if contact is to be in the family home, that the parent at least visit the foster family home and try to give some sense of it being 'okay' for the children to be there before the foster carer takes the children for a contact at their parents' home. Psychologically this is important for the child because, if a foster carer supervises contact at or drops children off at their family home it can be very difficult to get them back to the foster home without a lot of upset an hour or two later. When contact is supervised by social workers at a specialised unit, the parent leaves before the child is put into the car and returned to the foster carer. This can still be upsetting to the children but much easier for the workers to manage.

The social worker had made all of these decisions without any apparent consideration on the impact it could have on any fostering family and there was to be no discussion at the start of the placement about it because it was too late in the day and the following day the social worker would not be in the office and then the weekend was upon us. This was a social worker I had not yet met, as he worked out of an office in an area from which we had not had children placed with us before. Phil was the second male social worker I had worked with though and I hoped things would be as smooth as the last time, where the social worker, Kevin, turned out to be one of the nicest social workers you could have for discussions and debate. Kevin had also valued the carers he had children placed with and supported them very well, making sure they not only had him available to listen to concerns, but also had whatever equipment was needed for the job in hand, whether that was beds, prams or larger items of furniture.

Discussion and debate is a vital part of the job that foster carers do. Foster carers need to know that if they have an opinion it will be listened to and discussed. Whether the foster carers opinion gets acted on or not, at least they will have had their input as a valued (hopefully) member of the child's support team and can be given the reasons for whatever course of action follows.

So, here we were at the tail end of January with a cold wet and windy weekend ahead of us when the two children arrived. It was now after six on a Thursday evening and I had been expecting them to arrive since lunchtime.

When I opened the door I was faced with a rather tall exceptionally skinny and unkempt man who appeared to be slightly the worse for drink. With him were two scrawny little boys and a rather stout woman who, from her appearance could not possibly be related to or have anything to do with this little family, as she was so very well dressed but, she turned out to be the father's sister. One of the little boys was called Jake and was aged two years and the baby called Sam who was just coming up to his first birthday, though they both looked to be no more than mere bags of bones, much as their father was to be honest and just as unkempt and grubby looking.

We never keep people on the doorstep so they quickly came inside and introductions were done before we went into the lounge to discuss the boy's routines and get the children a little accustomed to their new home. Our children had all disappeared off to their rooms to have their own chat about the new arrivals and the people who had bought them to us. Certainly this wasn't a sight they had seen before. They had been more used to the children arriving with either a social worker or social services support worker, not the children's own family, and of course, there were also the little ones that had materialized over the years while our children had been sleeping peacefully through the night.

Steve, the children's father followed me into the lounge with the baby, Sam in his arms while Jake walked beside him. Steve's sister Sharon followed the little group. Howard was already in the kitchen putting the kettle on so the adults could have a hot drink and discuss the children's routine and their likes and dislikes while the children had a bedtime drink before their dad settled them into bed.

Well, that had been my plan but the state the children arrived in and the state their dad was in I figured he would be long gone before the children were ready for bed. He appeared too drunk to be of any use to us or his children at that time and his sister didn't offer to help and certainly didn't look the sort to dirty her pretty hands with grubby child care duties! I was trying not to judge but, at the end of the day everyone spends their life judging things, situations and people. This little group had me pretty stumped though.

It was an awkward first meeting with Sharon and Steve. Sharon kept saying she was in no position to help her brother as she had her own family to bring up and she didn't feel her home was suitable for two small children. I felt quite sorry for her as she seemed so genuine in her concern for her brother and nephews, but first impressions can be deceiving and we would soon learn exactly how Sharon felt about her nephews. I never worked out quite what she felt for her brother, though if she loved him I have often wondered how she could possibly have been so very cruel towards him at times during the following months.

I asked Steve if the boys had any routines that they followed at home and he gave a shrug, saying he wasn't sure what they did during the day, not knowing what time they got up or went to bed or even if they had an afternoon nap time. I asked about their diet, what foods they liked and disliked but he said he didn't have any idea what they ate or drank, or even at what times they had their meals, so it was going to be quite a learning curve, as was usual when children joined our family, while we discovered things about them, their likes and dislikes, tears, tantrums and happiness, and they learned all about us.

The only thing Steve was definite about was that both children would happily sleep whenever they were put to bed, day or night, if we wanted a bit of peace and quiet all we had to do was put them to bed, and that Jake had nursery school the following morning.

We had learned since we started fostering that many children will sleep when put to bed. This was possibly a coping strategy that even very young children use to escape their everyday lives. At least in sleep you can be at peace. In sleep, if your dreams are kind to you, you can be anywhere, with anyone and anything. I was and am always surprised at how young a child could be to use this as a means of escape…and saddened by it as well.

When I asked what Jake and Sam had eaten for their evening meal that day Steve said they had a 'bit of a sandwich' around one o clock but nothing since, and wasn't even aware of whether they had eaten anything earlier in the day. As it was quite a bit after six o clock by then I suggested Steve and his sister go home so I could get the children fed and into bed. Sharon quickly got her coat on and ushered Steve out of the house, saying to him that we had things to do and it would be best if they went quickly before the children became upset. Steve was very emotional at this point and said he would call in the morning. Jake and Sam were quite passive and just remained in the lounge as their dad and aunty went on their way and appeared to be completely unconcerned that they were being left behind with us.

Once we were on our own I quickly cooked up a small meal for the children of fish fingers chips and beans which they both ate, then Howard ran their bath and helped me to get them ready for bed. We noticed as they played in the bath that they both had quite extended stomachs, Sam more so than Jake and they were both extremely thin. Jake, the oldest, had a bruise at the bottom of his bony spine and Sam had what appeared to be bruising to his ankles. Jake also had a mark on his forehead that was two to three inches long, though how long it had been there was any ones guess.

Neither Jake nor Sam complained as they played and splashed around in the bubbles when we got them bathed and both also remained passive as we then got them changed into clean nightclothes ready for bed, then they both snuggled down with their new 'cuddle*' and the comfort blanket which they had both arrived with and settled to sleep immediately. Jake woke briefly a few hours later and asked for a bottle of juice but he settled quickly without the juice but happily had a cuddle instead.

Once Jake and Sam had settled and our children were occupied (and Howard was settled in front of the television) I telephoned Elizabeth, another foster carer who was also a very dear and close friend, to let her know about the boys. I knew she would be waiting for this call because we always kept each other in the loop with our placements. We were each other's first point of support if we had any problems that needed a second opinion and, if a large family needed placing it was nice if they were divided between our family and Elizabeth's family, space permitting, as that would mean they would have daily contact with each other because our families met up every day.

---

* *We always made sure every child coming to share our home had a soft toy that they could cuddle up to when they went to bed because we knew, even those that were 'to old and strong to be bothered by all this shite' probably needed something to hug even if they wouldn't admit to that need.*

Anyway, I told Elizabeth that, most unusual, the children were a local family and was chatting away about what lovely little lads they seemed to be when Elizabeth suddenly said 'You've got the gun siege family!' I didn't have a clue what she was talking about and just laughed, asking her what on earth she was talking about and, to be honest, dismissing the comment as her having a bit of a joke. But she persisted and told me the name of the road that the gun siege family lived in. I was shocked to say the least when it sunk in that Elizabeth knew so much about the children we had just had placed with us, as I hadn't been given this information from anyone in social services when I had been asked to take in the children. Elizabeth didn't have much information to hand about the case but had read about them a week or two earlier in a local paper and it was so surprising to have this sort of incident in our quiet little village that it had stuck in her mind. I didn't have much to go on…but I'd be speaking with social services and Phil, the children's social worker, in particular as soon as possible about this because the parents had our address and we were living so close to their family home.

Howard and I discussed our concerns about the children as they slept; they both had quite a few bruises on their little bodies, and they didn't appear to be the sort consistent with normal child play, considering their ages; They both appeared to be malnourished and Sam was quite lethargic. Also, considering their ages, Howard and I had been surprised while unpacking the few items that came with them, that all the toys they had were aggressive toys; tanks, soldiers and monsters. Having also given Howard all the information that Elizabeth had told me, we also spoke at length about our not being informed about any gun siege that had happened recently, which the social workers should have known about as the police had become involved at that time.

Chapter 3

The following morning the children woke at six fifteen. It was only thirty minutes earlier than our alarm normally went off, but we had quickly got used to having those thirty minutes back since the end of our last placement. We knew they would probably be lost for a while as these children and our family settled into what would be the norm for as long as our new additions shared our family life.

I got up and started my day with a quick shower before making Jake and Sam's breakfast and, when Edward, James and Claire came down, got theirs prepared for them as well. I loved being a mum and still got up and made our children's breakfast even though they were old enough and well able and capable of doing their own. There was the usual cacophony of childish banter as they bustled around getting everything they needed ready for school and Howard got ready for work, then, once Jake and Sam were fed washed and dressed our children kept an eye on the little ones as I got myself dressed and ready for the school run.

Once our children were at school, I walked home with Jake and Sam and prepared Jake for his nursery session (in those days we had nurseries and play schools where the children learned to socialize with their peer group. Nowadays it is called pre-school and they learn computing and writing) and started making phone calls to book appointments for the little ones to have their fostering medicals and to speak with their social worker to discuss the day to day managing of this placement.

I had found out that Phil not only worked from an office miles away, but also ran a social services support clinic each week from a room in our local children's clinic, so if I needed to speak to him and couldn't reach him by telephone, at least I knew he was only walking distance away on that one day.

Jake attended the nursery school which was run by social services. All local authorities have their own nurseries which are staffed by qualified social workers and are for children considered to be at potential risk of abuse. Sadly, with the rise in one parent families where the main parent possibly has multiple partners, there has been a rise in all sorts of abuse from physical to sexual and of course, neglect, which in many cases can be fatal, as these young parents search for fun and happiness and forget that they have a young child to care for and to consider, as they try to live the life of the carefree teenager which many of them should have still been.

Not all abuse is intentional though so some of these places are used by children whose parents have limited parenting skills due, possibly, to their own upbringing or simply because their parents live in an area where there are no extended family members to give a supporting hand when needed. And of course, not all of the country's single parents are party animals, some are simply just too young to have learned most of the skills needed to raise a child and maintain boundaries which make a child feel safe and secure.

Jake attended the nursery because social services became involved with the family when he was quite young and Jane, his mother, was struggling to manage with her two daughters and a demanding baby. Initially support was offered via social worker visits on a fairly informal basis while assessments were being made. When Sam was born and Jane found it harder to manage, it had been decided to offer Jake a place so he could be monitored as well as learn to have peer relationships and Jane would have a few hours respite each week, giving her time to bond with Sam and get some household chores done in relative peace while her daughters were at school.

I had been to one session of this nursery several years earlier so understood some of the concerns that the social services had for removing the children. One day a week (usually a Monday) at this nursery, all the children stripped down to their birthday suit and had a whale of a time playing in the paddling pools that were put up in the large play room. It was during this water fun time that the supervising social workers observed the children's bodies as well as their behaviour. Many children would have fresh bruising which looked non-accidental or were in areas that could be associated with child sex abuse. A doctor (who would be on site that day) would be called into the room so he could also observe from a distance, and then, if need be, check the children, before action was taken later that day if he considered it necessary to remove a child to a place of safety. I don't believe this water play happens nowadays, but it appeared to be a good, non-invasive method of checking up on what a child may be going through within their homes.

Jake's nursery time for that day was in the morning and a social worker would be collecting him. Once Jake was off I had a few hours just to play with and observe Sam. He was such a little cutie and very good, certainly appearing to be enjoying the time we had alone together. This little man was such a pleasure to be with, he looked like he was having fun playing with the toys and was very receptive to physical contact, appearing to be enjoying all the cuddles he got.

Sam's appetite I had noticed the previous evening and during breakfast that morning was quite good, but small so he would need to have a couple of snack meals in between his proper meals, something I didn't normally encourage but we had to try to get this child's weight up a bit and help his appetite to grow. Sam seemed to enjoy everything that was placed in front of him no matter what it was and eagerly accepted a mid-morning snack before having a short sleep while we waited for Jake to arrive home for lunch.

I had a surprising report from Jake's nursery nurses when he got home that day. They commented on the fact that he had good 'colour' in his cheeks and how he had been very well behaved, apparently so much so that it had been commented on by more than one member of staff, I was thrilled but wondered how one night away from his birth family could make such a difference and work such miracles!

I was assured though by the social worker that some children had such turbulent and disruptive home lives that even the one night of sleeping somewhere that felt safe, was enough to start quite drastic changes in young children's behaviours.

It's always nice to be told you have made a positive difference to someone's life, even if you have done so without noticing it.

I had been very lucky that morning and while Sam had napped I'd telephoned our surgery and had managed to get an appointment to see the doctor later that afternoon so, once I had met our children from school we all walked to the surgery. Edward, James and Claire waited in the waiting room while I took Jake and Sam in to have their medicals.

The doctor commented on both Jake and Sam's distended stomachs and noted with concern a bruise at the bottom of Jake's spine, but it was Sam's medical that was the most concerning. Poor little Sam had bruising to the head which, though faint with age was still visible. He had the remnants of a black eye with quite a large bump above it and, possibly the most concerning of all were the bruises to his abdomen which could be consistent with being pinched or picked up by the skin of his stomach. The doctor advised me to make another appointment to visit him in a couple of weeks so he could monitor the boy's weight and suggested a weekly weigh-in with the health visitor at the clinic as well, for both children. It was quite normal to have babies weighed in every week at the clinic, but once a child reached Sam's age, and certainly before Jake's age, these weigh-ins were down to once a month and then stopped all together by the time a child reached play-school age, so the fact we had to visit the clinic weekly was a bit concerning.

All of this I reported to Phil, the social worker, when I finally managed to speak to him as his working day drew to an end. It was fortunate I had managed to get hold of him then as today was Friday and he told me he had arranged for Jake and Sam's mother and their sisters to visit them at our home on Saturday morning for two hours. The family were arriving at about 10am, and then the boys would be spending time with their dad in the afternoon from 2.30pm at our home for two hours, where I would be supervising the contact, but then Jake and Sam would be going out with their dad for the whole day on the Sunday, leaving home at 10am and returning in time for bed.

I had never before worked with a social worker who kept me so out of the loop that the first I would have learned of these arrangements would have been when the mother and siblings turned up or Steve arrived on the doorstep, had I not made that telephone call. I explained to Phil my concerns regarding the state Steve had been in when he dropped the children off the previous evening but was told not to be so concerned and that it was probably a one off event. It was the end of what had been a stressful week for everyone so he told me to just make the most of the arrangements that had been made and enjoy the weekend. I was left with the feeling that I should be glad to have a few hours on Sunday without the 'borrowed' children around irrespective of my concerns regarding their safety.

It was only after the telephone call had ended that I remembered that I'd not mentioned anything about the gun siege to Phil, and he was, according to reception when I called back a few minutes later 'out of the office now'. It would have to wait until next week before we would be given additional information from social services regarding this issue and what bearing it may have on the case.

Chapter 4

Saturday morning came and went with no sighting of Jane, the boy's mother, or their sisters, nor did she phone to cancel the arrangements Phil said he had made.

This is a big problem with the support network put in place by social services. Once the working day or week is over you can't reach anyone directly involved with your child's case, you can only speak to an emergency social worker who you have possibly never met before and who has no idea what case you are working on nor the circumstances surrounding the children sharing your home. What if the children's mum had arrived on the Saturday morning? Had I not made that telephone call to the social worker I'd have had no idea whether to let her in or not; nor would a duty officer.

So, while Phil was having his weekend doing whatever he wanted, our family, like many other fostering families, were left in limbo not knowing if the mother would turn up at some time during the day, or even during the afternoon when Jake and Sam were to be spending time with their dad. And, if she did turn up then, what problems could we be facing and what may the repercussions be for the children and our family if the parents started an argument?

I have to be honest and say that, despite concerns that Jane may arrive at any time, we had a lovely lazy and relaxed morning that day. The little ones slept until after eight, with Jake sleeping until after nine and then both children playing nicely with our children and the toys. Howard and I were just hoping, partly in light of what we had found out the night before, that Steve would also forget any arrangements that had been made but, just after we had eaten our lunch he arrived and Jake became an absolute nightmare running around and jumping on the furniture shouting and screeching at the top of his voice before everyone settled down for the afternoon, with Steve chatting with us and playing with his children.

Howard and I had already decided we would not say anything about the gun siege incident to Steve or Jane if they arrived to spend time with their children unless they said something about it, opening the topic for conversation. Well, with Jane being a 'no-show' and Steve not mentioning it, the subject was left for me to discuss with Phil first thing Monday morning - providing I could get hold of him then of course.

Watching Steve playing with his sons was interesting because from his appearance – unwashed, unshaved and wearing tatty, creased and dirty clothes - you wouldn't really want to get too close to him and most people possibly wouldn't imagine him playing nicely and gently with little ones. It just showed one should never judge a book by its cover. Also, the way Steve played wasn't what I would expect when looking at the aggressive big boy toys that had arrived with them and that were now boxed up in the cupboard out of the way while they played with age appropriate toys. Steve appeared totally at home on the floor with the children and they responded positively towards him as they shared toys, cuddles and lots of laughter.

Steve apologised to us for the state he looked and explained that he had nowhere to stay at the moment and only had the clothes he stood up in, as the rest of his belongings were in the house he had been living in up until the previous day, when he had left with the children. He said he had spent the night in his car and spent the morning sitting in a café with a cup of coffee waiting for the time to pass so he could see Jake and Sam. I wondered, but said nothing, as to why he wasn't staying with his sister who had looked well off enough to be able to at least give him settee space.

What I didn't tell Steve was that his sister Sharon had telephoned that morning to let me know how concerned she was about Jake and Sam. Sharon had told me that their parents would soon be coming down (from where I wasn't told) to help sort the whole horrible mess out…and then she went on to tell me that the family had apparently already discussed the option of the children being adopted by a 'nice' couple if Steve couldn't cope. Adoption was apparently considered a good idea by Steve's family because the children were young and attractive so therefore would be appealing to people looking for an instant family. I had been absolutely floored by her comments, knowing that if anything had happened to Howard and I that the last thing our family would allow was for our children to be adopted by anyone other than one of our siblings. Also, although I knew that Jane, the children's mother, couldn't cope and didn't want them at the moment for whatever reason, there had been no formal plan drawn up by the department regarding the long term care of the boys. I only knew that they were here for now and would be for at least a couple of weeks, after that who knew what would happen? Yet here was this woman telling me how she and Steve's family had discussed adoption…Wow!

I did however manage to discretely ask Steve how often he had a drink at home because Jake had asked our Edward, who was only twelve years old at that time, if he was drunk while they were watching television that morning, Edward quite rightly had come and told me because though he found the question funny he knew it may be relevant in the planning of who these children would live with were they to be returned to either parent. Steve explained to me that he liked a drink as it helped him to cope with everyday problems that had been surrounding him for a while within his family and home life, but that he didn't drink to excess. I had to accept what he said at that time and just wait to see what his future behaviour showed.

Steve arrived on time to collect Jake and Sam at 10.20am on Sunday morning as planned, looking clean as well as wearing fresh clothes. He told me as he came into our home that his sister was allowing him to stay with her for the time being, which was excellent news. After a quick chat he took the boys out for the day, returning at teatime. I had suggested they came home earlier than the bedtime that Phil had said so that they could have a meal and then a relaxed bath and water play rather than just home, change and bed, feeling that this would be better for the boys. Steve had also jumped at the chance to help with the boys' bedtime routine, which was a positive in our eyes.

My concerns about Steve were eased a bit by the response from the children when he had arrived to collect them, well, Jake's reaction, as Sam was quite young and seemed to react the same to everyone who gave him a hug. Jake just seemed so absolutely overjoyed to see his dad again and, when they returned Steve spent time settling his children back into our home, chatting to them as Jake ate and he fed Sam. Once they were all ready for bed and it was time for him to leave, Steve reassured them he would see them again in two days. It was nice to see Steve explain clearly to Jake when he would next visit, he didn't just say 'I'll see you on Tuesday', he clearly explained to Jake, 'Tomorrow is Monday which is day one and then I will see you on Tuesday which is day two.' Once Steve had left, the children had their bedtime story and settled quickly to sleep once in bed.

Chapter 5

On the Monday, following a good night's sleep and a hearty breakfast, Jake went off happily to his play school.

Once Jake had gone and while Sam was playing quietly with some baby toys, I phoned Phil and asked him why he hadn't seen fit to tell me about the gun incident at the children's family home. Phil sounded amazed at the information I gave him, telling me he had no idea or information about it himself, but assured me that he would look into it as a matter of urgency because Jane still had her daughters living in the house with her and the social services would need to know if they were in danger of harm. I reminded him that we not only needed to know that Jake and Sam would also be safe when going out with Steve, but that everyone would be safe if either parent was going to be visiting our home to see the children.

Sometimes, although it was early days for this placement, it seemed that the most important person involved in all this was Jane and that meeting her needs was more important than meeting those of the children. Every time Phil spoke of Jane it was to praise her or excuse her behaviour, yet when he mentioned Steve it was always to condemn him as a useless person who was going nowhere.

This new information about the gun siege that I had passed on to Phil was so urgent and important to him that I heard nothing more about it and, as events unfolded and progressed within our home it was soon pushed to the back of our minds and forgotten by us as well. Although many, many months later when chatting with Phil he claimed to have found no information out anyway.

I had just put the phone down from talking to Phil when Sharon telephoned and asked me to re-affirm to Phil, or anyone higher up in social services, that her view and that of the family was for the children to be adopted by a nice young couple. I asked her if Steve was aware of the choices that his family were making for him and his children but was told quite bluntly that it would be for the best and that he would understand this in the fullness of time because he was in no position to care for Jake and Sam himself…and of course there was no family member willing or able to take the children in.

I had already spoken with Phil and told him about this discussion earlier that morning and, like me, he had been very surprised that the family had so quickly decided to dump the children and run for the hills so to speak. Phil seemed to be as confused and concerned as I was that there were conflicting views from Sharon regarding the children's future, depending on if Steve was within earshot or not. I told Sharon that I had already passed on her message from the other night regarding Jake and Sam's future as far as the family were concerned and told her that it was far too early in the placement for such choices to be made. I explained that there would need to be various assessments and numerous meetings of professionals before any decision was made. Sharon simply responded that the sooner things were finalised the better.

The day passed with the children eating, playing and enjoying the walk to collect James and Claire from school, visiting a couple of shops en route to buy some new clothes and toys for them. Our children, as always, had already fallen into what would be our normal routine now we had extra little ones living with us and spent time, once homework had been done, playing with and amusing Jake and Sam while I got on and prepared our evening meal.

During the early part of the evening Steve phoned to confirm that he would be seeing his children the following day. It sounded like he was calling from a pub but I was busy with our family so didn't ask him what he was doing or where he was and, at the end of the day, it was none of my business what he did when he didn't have the children with him. A little later on that evening, Steve's mother phoned to say she would be 'coming down' on Thursday and informed me that she felt Jane was taking hard drugs (though didn't say why she thought this, just that it was the type of thing a person like Jane was probably doing). This was something else to pass on to Phil in the morning, not only the possibility that Jane may be taking drugs but also the amount of hostility from Steve's family towards her. It would probably have benefited the whole family if instead of rallying round to get rid of the children now, the extended family members that were most vocal had actually managed to physically and emotionally put support in place earlier.

I listened to Steve's mother and thought how like her daughter she was with all the negative things she said about Jane, the mother of two of her grandchildren, and wondered how any grandmother could sit by if she thought her grandchildren were being mistreated. Surely I thought (naively as my upbringing had been so lovely), most extended family members, and especially parents, only want for their children to be happy as adults and would make attempts to at least try to like whoever their child chose as a partner and parent for their children; even if, behind closed doors away from that person their true feelings came out.

Later that night Steve phoned again…this time he sounded quite drunk. Steve slurred his words as he told me he wouldn't be going back to Jane even though she wanted him back. Steve rambled on, some quite incoherent sentences tumbled from his mouth. He clearly told me though that Jane would try to use the children to get him back, then he changed that to 'get back at me.' I tried to advise Steve to take any counselling that was offered to him and he agreed to do anything, but refused to even consider family therapy. Steve rambled on that his children were everything to him and that if it was considered best for them to be 'elsewhere' then that's what should happen…following up with the sentence "even if I commit Hara-kiki afterwards".

I knew as soon as that sentence was uttered that he had spoken to his family and that they had told them what they felt would be the best course of action for his children, and now he was quite emotional, totally drunk and in a telephone box somewhere on his own.

Steve was actually extremely emotional as well as very drunk. He told me it was because he had done a favour for some friends and they had all given him a drink to cheer him up…it clearly hadn't worked! We spoke for about half an hour with me trying to reassure him that his children would not just be placed for adoption with someone until after a full assessment of his abilities to care for his children had been carried out. Family members on both sides would also be approached to see if they could help. Steve was distraught and told me he'd had enough today with Jane giving him 'GBH of the earholes' and he just wanted to sleep, but assured me that he would try to be honest when talking to Phil and tell him everything about what the children's lives had been like so far. Then he rang off.

There was nothing we could do when we heard the line go dead. We had no idea where Steve was, only that he was alone, drunk and feeling emotional and tired. We hoped he would at least get somewhere warm before he went to sleep and then we had a very restless night ourselves worrying about him.

Chapter 6

I don't think I had ever been so pleased to see a birth parent as I was when Steve arrived the following morning. Relief that he was still alive and hadn't done anything stupid overnight drove me to have a few stern words with him, which he appeared to take well, though that may have been in order to escape with his headache and the boys as quickly as possible!

Considering how drunk he had sounded the previous night Steve appeared quite sober now, so I debated allowing him to take the children out with him once he'd had a cup of coffee and we had talked over not only the events of the previous night and how serious they were, but also talking about the children's futures, with me once again giving him reassurance that his children would not be placed for adoption without assessments being done on him and any family members who came forward and of course, pointing out his responsibilities toward the children which meant he should try to avoid visiting any pubs while he was looking after them for the day. I let Steve know that I was debating whether to allow his contact to be away from our home that day but, after assuring me that he wouldn't go near a pub while they were out I let the contact go ahead as planned.

My day was then spent trying to get straight and organized, sorting out what clothes and toys we still needed to purchase for the children as well as trying to work out how long this placement would last. From past experience and because of what I had heard and seen from the children, Steve and his family in the few days they had been sharing our home, I guessed it would be quite a long placement, one that would possibly be taking us through this year and into the early part of the following one before we had sorted out the mess that was the children's life to date, and started the work necessary to make their future a better one than it might have otherwise been.

I think it was fairly clear even at this early stage that Steve wanted to have his children living with him; he just didn't know how to do this. He appeared to be muddled and confused about which way to turn and who could he trust? His family clearly had little or no faith in his ability to care for the boys which seemed to make him 'know' he would muck up and lose them anyway. I know it was early days and I was making judgements (again), but I quite liked Steve. When sober, he appeared a quiet and gentle man with a sense of humour and a total commitment to his children. We just needed to find a way of not only caring for Steve's children while they were with our family...but also helping him to realise the answer to his problems did not lay in the bottom of a bottle or can. He also had to realise that he was the one who had work to do to convince the social services that he was the one who should have his children permanently in his life.

So, as well as looking after the children we set about helping Steve gain some much needed self-esteem and pride…no easy task for someone who was of no fixed abode, as already his sister had decided she didn't have space for him in her home and he was back sleeping in his car, which meant that the car was quite full with all his clothes and personal belongings as well as the children's car seats. There wasn't room to swing a cat in the car and one of the back windows was also broken so it was freezing inside.

Following their day out with their dad the boys looked happy but dirty when they got home and settled nicely after their evening routine of tea, bath and bedtime story from Howard saw them into their beds.

Howard and I chatted later that evening and decided we would have to at least offer Steve the opportunity of having a shower and change into fresh clothes when he arrived on the days he had contact with Jake and Sam; at least until he had somewhere to live. We would also invite him to join us for meals if it seemed appropriate when he returned with the children after taking them out for the day. The only thing we couldn't actually offer him was bed space…that would be a step too far as the children were living with us for a reason and they needed to be protected from whatever had been their life experience so far and we had to make sure we didn't blur boundaries too much.

To be honest, we shouldn't have been blurring the boundaries at all and had only known Steve for a short time but…and it was a big but…he seemed genuine and honest. He accepted the things he did wrong and even discussed them openly with us, asking for advice and so far, most advice appeared to have been taken and acted upon which is why we had decided to take a little step outside of our normal remit and went that extra mile now.

However, the next day I was going to hear and learn something, and I wouldn't like it one bit.

Chapter 7

I woke up early on the sixth day of this placement as Jake and Sam were to spend the day with their mother and they had another medical to attend late in the afternoon. They hadn't seen their mum since they had arrived and I hadn't said anything to Jake in case she didn't show up again today so as not to upset him. I got everything that would be needed for the day sorted and packed before getting the children up, so Jake wouldn't ask why I was putting a change of clothes, food, nappies and toys into the bag that was used when they went out with their dad for the day.

Jane arrived at 10.30am as arranged...Sorry but...I thought 'Damn'...shame about that but such is life and they are her kids.

The first thing Jake said to her, before anything else was 'Has dad hit you?'

I was shocked. It hadn't occurred to me that Steve would be a wife beater!

Jane didn't answer Jake and he didn't go to her, just stood and watched. Considering the question he had just asked his mum, I would have expected him to go for a hug or to at least offer a her hug, because it appeared to have been a question asked out of concern, even from one so young but Jake's behaviour and reaction to his mum was the polar opposite to that of when his dad arrived to see him. There had been no excited whoop of pleasure and arms thrown up for a big bear hug when Jane arrived…just a question followed by observation and silence.

Jane was very tearful on arriving at our home and, as she calmed down she told me that she only drank when Steve was there because she could then blot everything out…she said she loved her boys and wanted them back home…Now.

That was when I realised that I hadn't signed any paperwork…I didn't even know what sort of placement this was…it could be just respite; or short term…or…voluntary, in which case she could just walk out of the door with her children and I wouldn't be able to do anything about it.

Now, with a respite placement you have the children for a few hours, days or weeks until a minor blip in the family home is resolved. With a short term placement you have the children while a problem is resolved and the children then return home or move in with extended family until any issues are sorted out or, as sometimes happened, it could slip into a longer term placement and you would have the children until their future was secured through long term care or adoption…or they eventually went home. But with voluntary care, the parents can just take the children home whenever they choose as there is no court order saying they can't...and at that point, I had no idea what I would do if Jane just tried to walk away with her children.

Jane told me the children were with us because it was what she and Steve had chosen to do, place their children in voluntary care. I managed to speak with Phil and he confirmed what Jane had said. This placement was fostering on a voluntary basis so Jane could just take the children and walk any time she pleased.

I suggested to Jane that she spoke to Phil regarding any counselling or therapy that was available to her, which would help her come to terms with past events and help her cope with her present problems before taking the boys home for good. I was concerned at this point that she was discussing Steve and his family in front of Jake who, though now playing with toys could still hear what was being said, though of course I didn't know what his understanding would be. Jane had nothing but anger and animosity for Steve's family and in particular for Sharon, who she seemed to have known for some time as Jane appeared to hold her responsible for the breakdown of her first marriage.

I didn't know until then that Jane had been married previously or anything else about Jane except that she had two little girls from an earlier relationship and two little boys from her relationship with Steve. She did make it absolutely clear that the girls were so very important to her...and though the boys came second, she would still like them back.

Jane left with the boys and I had a sinking feeling that they would not be sleeping here that night, though she had agreed to bring Jake and Sam back to our home later that day so at least the children could have their medicals.

I spoke to Phil as soon as Jane and the children had left to explain my concerns and he just told me to let the boys go back to her if that's what she wanted…I could only hope that he would be hard at work in the background, getting paperwork typed up for court which would bring Jake and Sam under the umbrella of 'looked after by the local authority' via an interim care order, so that Jake and Sam could be protected from whatever was going on within their parents relationship and all the issues that came with it, and be properly cared for while a full assessment was carried out on every adult that wanted to be the main carer for Jake and Sam as, in my mind, an assessment was very clearly needed. Though also going through my mind was that the only person who appeared to really want these children living with them was Steve, but dads didn't seem to have the same 'rights' that mums had.

I met with Jane later that afternoon in the street. She hadn't arrived back at our home with the children as had been arranged earlier in the morning, so I had decided to call around to her house to ask if they could at least have their medical carried out which she had agreed to earlier that day. I explained that a medical would show that they were fit and healthy right now, and didn't say anything about them possibly having another medical after she had them home for a few days which may show up some different issues.

Jane told me she was on her way to our house when we met up and, though she wasn't happy, she agreed I could take Jake and Sam to the doctor but only if I promised to take them straight back to her house afterwards...Bugger...I had to make that promise or she would just turn and walk away now and we needed to know that the boys were okay...I made the promise and walked off towards the village. I also knew I had to honour my promise or there would never be any chance of having a good working relationship with Jane once the children did return to our home, something I knew would happen at some point in time, if not later that day.

Following the visit to the doctor I walked slowly to Jane's house. The doctor had been concerned that some of the bruising was NAI (non accidental injury)...and here I was being forced to take the children back to someone who may have been instrumental in causing them harm. At the very least, she hadn't protected the children from receiving the injuries. There were just so many concerns going through my mind about this little family because, although it was only Jake and Sam that had been living with us, there were also two little girls living in the family home and surely, I thought, they may also be at risk of some sort of abuse.

This was in the days that not everyone had a mobile phone so, though Steve had one, I didn't and I would just have to wait until I got home before speaking to Phil about my concerns and see what the next step would be. I couldn't go home before taking the children to Jane's house in case she saw me and accused me of breaking my promise. Much as I would have liked to speak with a social worker as soon as possible, I would just have to bide my time, maybe have a cup of tea with Jane and see how the boys reacted to being in their own home again and watch how they interacted with their sisters and their mum.

We had always, as foster carers, to assess every situation and report back to the social worker what we saw and what we felt, though these were two very different things because what you see is fact, what you feel is personal to you and may not actually be relevant to the social worker or their plans for the children involved.

I hoped I would be able to convince Jane to let me take the children home again once she had seen them. I knew I couldn't tell her that the doctor had concerns about the injuries he had found. That would be for Phil to discuss with her at some point and the sooner that happened, the better as far as I was concerned.

Jane's house was chaotic. I was invited in for a cup of tea which I accepted because, although it was chaotic and extremely untidy, it looked fairly clean in the kitchen. Jake and Sam were both clearly distressed within moments of our arrival, and Jake started rummaging through the fridge freezer for food. Jane told him she would cook sausages for tea then proceeded to make cheese sandwiches...Jake called her a 'Fucking wanker' and Sam tried to remove part of the door on the washing machine which he had crawled over to. While this chaos was going on downstairs, I could hear Jane's daughters screaming and squealing and bouncing around upstairs and on the stairs as they ran all over the house.

Jane made allegations against Steve's sister, saying Sharon allowed her children to watch sexual intercourse between her and her husband. While discussing this with me she was trying to feed bits of fruit to Jake and Sam to keep them quiet, the cheese sandwiches having been forgotten, so I would hear what she was saying. I did my best to convince Jane it was in the children's and her best interests to allow me to take the Jake and Sam home with me, which would allow her time to think through what the best possible outcome in the long term would be for everyone, including her daughters.

Jane's little girls had started arguing and the boys were crying and Jane looked and said she felt very tense. She then simply said she would give them some sweets to shut them up and asked me to leave as she showed me the door...Poor Jake and Sam were still crying behind me as I had to walk away.

It was now too late to speak with Phil as the office was closed, so I just hoped again that he had been busy getting the paperwork typed up ready to go to court the next day.

Later that evening Steve phoned...it sounded like he was in the pub and he already knew the children were not here. He said he wouldn't go to the family home that night and hoped the boys would be back with us in the morning. He wasn't the only one. I guess at least we now knew there was some communication going on with Jane and Steve, we just weren't sure if this was a good thing or not.

Steve's mother also telephoned later that evening to make more allegations,. This time she accused Jane of leaving the children alone for hours on end and she asked for the emergency social worker number 'in case it is needed.' Though how she would know if it was needed I wasn't sure because she didn't live anywhere near Jane and wasn't on speaking terms with her at that time. It seemed as though Steve's family didn't want the children's mum or dad to be involved with their children as they grew up…something the paternal family didn't appear to want for themselves either.

Over the years we have fostered, I have often pondered on the allegations people make about their partner or family members…it was almost as though, while Steve and Jane were together it was okay for the children to be left alone for hours and to have a (supposedly) drug taking mother…but now Steve wasn't living with them they had to be supervised at all times…also, did Jane condone the behaviour she accused her sister-in-law of, or had she reported her before? So much hatred and anger had burst out in a few days it was hard to sort truth from malicious fiction on both sides of this family group. The only thing I felt really sure of at that time was that Jake had, at some time in his short life, witnessed Steve hitting Jane and, though I would never condone physical violence between people…I wondered, having spent time with him and Jane, what had driven him to that action?

Chapter 8

The following morning the health visitor arrived to see Jake and Sam. I explained that they were still at their mothers so we sat and discussed the case, as she would become involved when they eventually returned to the care system, which everyone knew was only a short time away...but for now, because the children were based with a different family doctor when living in the family home, they belonged to a different health visitor so mine could do nothing apart from make her colleague aware of concerns my doctor had raised.

Jane arrived unannounced at 1.00pm with Jake and Sam. I was surprised and pleased to see her and invited her in for a coffee. She agreed to come in for a quick cuppa so she could let me know what she had decided regarding the children. We had a long chat while Jake played in the playroom and Sam slept in the pushchair. I told Jane that it looked like her and Steve were in self-destruct mode and that they only seemed happy when scoring points off each other. This was not a good place for any of the children to be...a virtual marital war zone. Jane said she desperately wanted Steve to come home because it was just too hard coping with four children on her own…then she suddenly said she never wanted to see him again. I was concerned about Jane's mental health at this point as she appeared to be bouncing off all the walls and changing her mind in the blink of an eye…Then Steve telephoned.

While I had Steve on the phone I managed to get talking to both of them about their relationship and, amazingly, they agreed to both come to our home the following Monday at lunchtime to discuss with me and the social worker where they felt this case should go and what help they both needed to get there.

What a result!

Now all I had to do was ensure Phil would also be at our home as Jane had, for now, agreed to do anything Phil suggested…as long as Steve didn't take Jake and Sam to Sharon's house…my goodness, she had such a total loathing for her sister-in-law.

As nice as the afternoon was for the boys while their mum and I chatted, it came to an end all too soon and Jane left, having explained that she was taking the children with her for now, but letting me know she would return them if they got too much over the next three days…she also confirmed again that she would definitely turn up on Monday to speak with Phil, Steve and me.

I only hoped she would remember.

Of course, this meant that our family would be quite limited on what we could do and where we could go over the weekend as we had to be on stand-by in case Jane returned the children to our home. Such is the life of a fostering family.

I let Phil know what had been arranged and hoped it didn't interfere with any schedule he had. I don't think he was best pleased to know I'd made these arrangements without any discussion with him but, as the deed was done he agreed to be at my home in plenty of time for a chat before the meeting started. I hoped that he would not be so cross come Monday as he sounded during that telephone call and of course, that he would arrive with any paperwork needed to bring the children back into the safety net of the local authority.

Chapter 9

Following a quiet few days with no contact from social services, Jane or Steve, Phil arrived at midday on the Monday. We were now twelve days into the placement and this was the first time I had physically met the children's social worker. He was certainly a breed apart from the others that I had met.

Phil walked into our lounge and seemed to fill the whole room up…not just because he was physically a big bloke, but because he had an ego and personality as broad as his shoulders! Normally a social worker would say 'hi', 'hello' or 'how's things going' and then sit and chat until the meeting started…not so with Phil. With Phil it was full on body hug…a huge bear hug and then the introductions of 'Hi…I'm Phil'…Phil gave me a short history of himself…and we shall come to that later in the book…

Okay, so Phil is a short round bear of a man who is very hands on friendly with his foster carers…I could only sit back and hope he was as friendly and persuasive with his clients and we could then get the kids back here with me today. Unfortunately the paperwork had not hit the court arena yet, but Phil said it was all ready to go.

Jane and Steve arrived just before 12.30pm, Steve arriving first and then Jane bringing the boys in with her. Once the initial excitement of seeing their dad and the toys in the playroom had settled down, Jake happily went off and played in the playroom and Sam slept contentedly for the duration of the meeting, neither showing signs of not wanting to be here.

Jane eventually agreed that Jake and Sam would return to our home that afternoon. The choice she had been given was to either return them voluntarily, or the paperwork was ready to go to court in the morning and there would then be an interim care order placed on Jake and Sam. This would give both Steve and Jane far fewer rights than they had at that moment.

Sorted…also, they would both be offered counselling and parenting classes in order to be better able to care for and raise their family themselves. It was also agreed during the meeting that Steve could take the children to visit his parents for a long weekend the following week.

Once the meeting was over Jane left alone, having decided that it would be easier if she just left Jake and Sam with me then rather than take them home and have to return later. Phil also left, which meant that Steve could relax and stay for lunch and, once lunch had been eaten Steve took the boys out for the afternoon.

We had a lovely couple of hours as a family before Steve arrived back with the children in the early hours of that evening. We always valued the short times we had as 'just us' because it didn't happen very often and, much as our children never complained about sharing their home with other peoples kids…we still had to make sure they knew they were 'extra special' because they actually played a pivotal role in allowing us to work with the children and families that we worked with, even though they were too young to actually appreciate that fact at the time.

Steve had returned home with the children promptly at 5.00pm as he said he would, he didn't stay long and, though he was quite emotional and crying, the children settled quickly into the evening meal and bedtime routine that we had started at the beginning of the placement. Jake had quite sore looking eczema on his hand which had flared up in the past few days and looked like it needed treatment. It seemed pretty clear that he needed to be a lot less stressed if it was to clear up any time soon and the best way to de-stress a child is by having security in their life.

Once the little ones were settled in bed I left Howard with the children and went to collect some clothes from Jane's house, something that had been agreed on earlier in the day.

Jane made us both a coffee and we chatted while we gathered a few bits together. The house was still in total chaos, not with so much noise, but there was so much stuff just thrown everywhere…clothes, toys and food all over the floor and even in the wardrobes and opened drawers there were split packets of all sorts of food.

I had already been out and purchased several items of clothing so didn't need to take too much but took those bits offered so as not to cause any offence to Jane, though I knew as I left that it would be unlikely that I would use any of it even if it washed up ok because most of it looked either very old and shabby or just too small.

I know this probably sounds quite bad to most people who are reading this as the first Lizzie Scott book they have picked up but, as foster parents we were given an allowance to help towards the cost of clothes and toys for the children that were placed in our homes. I felt then, and still do now, that the quickest way to help build a child's self-esteem and make them feel like a valued member of your family, which has become their family by virtue of them moving into the family home, is by making them look like the rest of the people who live there. Not physically of course, but simply by wearing nice clean clothes that fit and having decent footwear on their feet. This works well with children who are of primary school age, though obviously you needed to tread a little more carefully with older children or they may think you just don't like their families. With most of the younger children we worked with I would tend to save the clothes that came from their home, if suitable, for when they had contact with their birth family, that way the birth family wouldn't feel offended, though some parents would get annoyed when you stopped sending the child in 'home clothes' because they had become too small, while others complained that their children should be wearing new clothes because 'foster carers are paid to dress my kids'.

So, back to the story…As Jane and I chatted over the coffee, the girls could be heard playing upstairs so it was fairly relaxed even though Jane was a little upset and emotional. She told me that she was relieved to have the boys back living with us as it had been very difficult trying to look after them on her own, but she felt guilty about it all the same. I told her not to feel guilty as lots of people need support at different times and to different levels…and she had no family living locally to help her out when things went belly up.

We finished packing the things I was to take with me and as I left, Jane promised again that she would do all that Phil asked of her and also that she would try not to argue with Steve. It was early days though, and we were all in for a few surprises from Jane surrounding the commitment to these children and honouring the plans that were to be put in place in order to secure a good and safe future for them.

I hadn't long arrived back home when Steve's mother phoned me and asked me to pass a message on to him when he next had Jake and Sam. I was to tell him the children had to be back here by Sunday evening and not Tuesday or Wednesday evening like Steve had asked for and which, after some discussion had been agreed with Phil at the meeting.

I guess all grandparents have their own lives to live as well…and of course, we didn't know what the children were like on 'extended family turf' so to speak, but I felt sorry that a grandmother could choose to spend such little time with her grandchildren.

I had hoped that when she 'popped down' she would have called in to meet her grandchildren's foster family and see Jake and Sam but she hadn't, so this would be the first time she had seen them in a few months. I hoped they would behave as well while with their grandparents as they did here, and maybe their grandmother would then decide to support Steve in his quest to become their full time dad.

Chapter 10

A few days after the meeting, I took the children to hospital for x-rays. This was necessary due to concerns from my doctor when he'd done the medicals...after this we had lunch then I dropped them off to their mum's house for contact, where they would be staying for tea before coming home. This was also the first time Jane had seen the children since leaving our home after agreeing that they could return to live with us.

Jane was quite concerned when she came in to drop the children off later in the day because Jake had told her they'd had their photograph taken by the doctor. Jane wanted to know why the children had to have their photographs taken...were the social services looking for evidence that she was a bad mother and were they also looking for old scars and bruises? I explained to her that it was x-rays that the children had been taken for and Jane became visibly even more concerned...Because of her reaction, so did I.

Just before leaving Jane told me that Steve had told her the previous night (I wondered if he had visited the family home or simply telephoned?) that the children should be with her and, if she had them back he would return to live with her as well…also, Jane said that if it had been her daughters in care she would have been tearing her hair out, but followed that comment by saying that she didn't seem really at all bothered about his (Steve's) sons being in the care system…sadly, once she told me that, she said she agreed with Steve's comment…she loved her boys but wasn't at all upset or bothered that they were living away from her and that she really didn't know now if she wanted them back ever.

Apparently Jake and Sam complicated things.

Jane was due to take the children out again the following day, but when she arrived to collect them she asked if they could just stay in our home for the duration of her contact. Jake and Sam were both having a nap when she arrived and I said I'd go wake them for her but was stopped when she said she'd rather they slept a little while longer.

We sat talking for an hour while we had a coffee. Jane appeared relaxed and had taken trouble over her appearance today, wearing a nice skirt and high heels. She talked about the stress she had been under recently and how relieved she was not to have to look after the boys (despite loving them very much). Jane talked a bit about her family and said how like her mother Sam looked…Jane's mother had died a while back, which was possibly why she felt 'un-bonded' to him. I suggested bereavement counselling to her and said I would discuss it with Phil when we next spoke if she wanted me to. This was agreed so I made a quick note to remind myself and made another coffee. Jane told me that she wanted Jake and

Sam to be placed back with her and her daughters, just that she didn't want it to happen at that time...her actual words being 'They stay here until I'm ready, with or without Steve.'

Jake and Sam eventually woke and spent a very short time with Jane as she had to go to collect her girls from school and I had to get to a different school to pick up James and Claire. I hadn't said anything to Jane about how Jake had become upset periodically during the morning and had been asking to go to 'mummy's house', and was surprised that he didn't once mention it himself while she was here as he could be fairly vocal with his views, even for one so young.

When it was time to go Jane did as I asked and simply said a quick goodbye to Jake and Sam then walked out the door...this made it easier for them to settle for the few minutes we had spare before we also left home to get down the road ourselves. Altogether, it had been quite a pleasant afternoon...aided I suspected, by Jake and Sam being asleep and allowing Jane time to relax and just talk about her life and her issues.

As she had said goodbye, Jane told Jake she would come and see him again the following day. It was five days before we heard from her or saw her again.

Steve telephoned later on that evening, he was sounding quite drunk and repeated almost word for word what Jane had said about if she had the boys return to live with her...only his term was 'I may come home.'

65

I guess we were quite lucky that the following day Steve was taking the children to visit his parents, so with the excitement of that, Jake appeared to forget about Jane popping in to see him and he went off happily enough with Sam in Steve's car...after the strong cup of coffee and another little talk about not being able to sort problems out by drowning them in alcohol. Howard and I do drink so I don't ever preach on this subject, but I just had to make sure Steve would be okay and safe while with the children and wouldn't be drinking and driving while he was away.

Two days later we had a telephone call from Steve's mother. She sounded tired and to be honest, quite relieved to say they were on their way home and, a couple of hours later they arrived back, with Steve complaining that Sam had spoiled what had been a great weekend for Jake by being miserable and getting up to all sorts of mischief. His behaviour, Steve said, had also made it hard work for his mother. Poor Sam, barely a year old and already he had been through so much before arriving in our home and, since sharing our lives he had yo-yoed back and forth between us and his mother then his grandparents. What could anyone expect from him? Certainly not any semblance of settled behaviour from such a short but unsettled life!

I guess for these children the constants were Howard and I...and Steve too because he appeared to be committed to seeing them daily when Jane and Phil allowed him to.

It looked like it had been a tough weekend on Jake as well because that night he wet the bed.

The next day, Monday, was a good day. Once Edward, James and Claire were at school I went straight home to spend some quality time with Jake and Sam. I guessed they just about needed to have some quiet safe time at home chilling out, playing and relaxing. However, Jake had other ideas. He was going to clarify something for me and give me something to think about…and something to make a quick call to Phil about as well.

We had been home playing with the bricks and small cars for about an hour and a half when suddenly Jake looked at me and said 'mummy had a gun'. I must have looked a bit surprised because he repeated himself about mummy having a gun then followed that up with the fact (as far as he was concerned) that she was going to kill him. I waited a moment but Jake resumed playing as though he hadn't said a word so I asked him what he meant…'Mummy has a gun and she's going to kill me' he repeated again…I reassured him that his mummy wouldn't kill him, though wasn't sure what his idea of being killed was and carried on playing with him in the hope he would say some more about this gun, like about where mummy kept it, but he didn't mention it again and I didn't want him to have guns and death on his mind all day so let the subject drop. I was glad he had said as much as he had to me because at least I could now let Phil know that Jake had also seen the gun…or had at the very least been told about it.

I phoned Phil a couple of hours later when I had time alone as I didn't want young ears picking up any concern from me but, if Jake said there was a gun I was inclined to believe him as kids his age don't usually make such random comments unless there is an element of truth in there somewhere. Phil amazingly was fairly dismissive of my concerns and told me he saw no reason for concern.

There may well have been no reason to think Jane would carry a gun and shoot anyone but surely of concern would be that a child had said such a thing. Why would a young child come out with such a random comment if it wasn't playing on his mind? Why would he say something like that if he hadn't seen the gun or at the very least heard comments about it? Didn't that alone warrant some sort of consideration?

I guessed Phil was just playing his cards very close to his chest, and certainly hoped he was. At the same time, it would have been nice if he had shown me some respect and consideration instead of appearing to mock me almost every time we spoke. I had a valid concern and wanted it accepted as such, especially as Jake and Sam had home contact with their mum.

Jane phoned the following morning and told me she was going to be having the boys for the day, assuring me she would return them in the afternoon, which she did, though Sam had been so irritable when she had arrived to collect them and had screamed and kicked so much that he'd had to be held while his coat was put on him and while he was strapped into the pushchair, that I thought she may just leave him here. Unfortunately she didn't leave him, insisting that he was just having a little temper tantrum.

When they returned early that evening Jane had her sister with her and looked quite annoyed about something but she just said she was feeling concerned about the meeting we were all to have later in the week to clarify how the case was moving along and to re-affirm the commitment expected from both parents regarding the children's future. Jane explained that as they were going out they would not stop for a coffee and to settle the children back in. Sam was quite subdued and irritable, wanting lots of cuddles and attention, but settled quickly into the evening routine once Jane and her sister had left.

The following day Steve had the boys, picking them up early and returning them after tea and just in time to be readied for bed. But of course, Jake had fallen nicely into his evening routine and wanted a nice warm bubble bath before getting his pyjamas on…so we noticed and recorded not only the scratches to his face, but also the bruising to the inside of his knees, which Steve explained was because he had kept falling over.

The next day Phil had arranged for Jane, Steve and me to meet in his office at the clinic to discuss the arrangements for contact and to look at how we could move forward with the children's lives.

The meeting was the most informal I had ever been to and I got the impression that, no matter what Jane did Phil would find a positive light to see it in. Jane was quite an attractive female and Phil was certainly a ladies man. Phil also wanted the children returned to Jane as soon as possible and appeared to want Steve out of the picture completely, which was a shame because the boys seemed to have a much better relationship with their dad than their mum. Also, there was the issue of the gun which wasn't even addressed. Jane agreed to everything that was put to her...she would go to parenting classes and would turn up for contact with Jake and Sam once it was finalised how many days contact each parent would have. Steve also agreed to do whatever was asked of him in order for him to have his sons sharing his life.

I definitely had the feeling that Steve was the more sincere of the parents in that room during the meeting and felt that his words were spoken with honesty while Jane's appeared to be hollow promises.

Later that day Jane came to our home to visit the children, bringing her daughters with her. Both Jake and Sam became very clingy towards me and moaned the whole time she was there. Jake managed to fall over and split his lip which caused utter mayhem and when, at 5.30pm I suggested an early bedtime for Sam who had cried almost from the moment his mother arrived I was met with a very firm 'yes please' from Jane and off he went to bed.

Jane had spent most of the time she was in our home complaining and rubbishing everything Steve had said at the meeting, especially the bits that involved being an active parent in his children's life, and repeated that she wanted to be physically and mentally strong before making any decision about Jake and Sam's future, stating that if they went home too soon she would slip back into her old ways. Then she added that her sister may move into her home to help look after the children. I wasn't sure what her 'old ways' were because I had still not received any paperwork on this family and we hadn't had a formal review.

This whole case was so unlike any other one I had worked on. There appeared to be no structure or even a semi solid-plan that everyone was working towards. It seemed as though we were just strolling around and seeing where we ended up.

The next day Jane once again visited Jake and Sam in our home, this time arriving at 3.30pm and bringing her daughters with her for tea. The children all ate nicely together and were quite well behaved except for Sam who, young as he was, aggressively said 'no' to everything his mother said, so in the end, once again I suggested he have an early night. Jane quickly agreed to this and asked me to get him settled while she stayed talking and playing with the older three children.

Once Sam was settled in bed and the older children were playing quietly Jane told me that Sam had always behaved badly at home and had never been what you would call a 'happy baby', unlike her daughters who were always so good.

Jane and I chatted for most of the time they were visiting, leaving Jake and his sisters to play with the toys and each other. Usually the idea of parental contact was for the parents and children to interact with each other while the foster carer observes, but Jane had very little to do with Jake and Sam at any of her contact visits in our home, always leaving personal care and floor play to me. This meant my only observation was that she didn't appear able to interact with her sons and in return, they appeared unable to interact with her.

Jane kept telling me that she was happy to accept any help that was being offered in order to have Jake and Sam back living with her and her daughters. She was also quite adamant that she didn't want Steve to play any part in her life anymore because she was afraid of him going to her house and said that it made having the boys home more difficult, as he would have to visit to see them and pick them up for contacts if she had them living with her and her daughters.

Jane also told me a little bit about her own childhood, about how her father was 'a right bastard to us kids' and how they used to run and hide on a Thursday night when he'd arrive home drunk. Jane appeared to be reflecting on her childhood and said that he was always drinking. Maybe, she said, that's where her problems started, though she quickly let me know that he had changed now and was okay as a dad.

Listening to Jane talk was quite interesting because, if Steve was the person she described him to be, she had indeed got involved with a man who was the mirror image of her father in personality if not in looks. She could well have continued feelings of anger towards him for anything he may, or may not have done if he'd had a drink, irrespective of how many and how drunk he became. I was listening and pondering what she was saying when she suddenly asked if she could take Jake out and leave Sam at home next time she visited. At the time, I felt that it would be beneficial to her and Jake to have a nice time without Sam as he clearly became very distressed in his mother's company so I agreed to her request, though told her I would have to run it past Phil, and just hoped that Phil would also see the merit in this action. It also meant that Sam would have my undivided attention for a couple of extra hours, something which he always seemed to enjoy when Jake was at playschool.

I had noticed that though Jane would sometimes cuddle Sam, she did so while being verbally very negative towards him and released her hold at the first opportunity, unlike when she cuddled Jake and spoke quite gently as well as making the contact with him last longer.

I felt so sorry for poor little Sam, because Steve, although he hadn't verbalized anything like Jane just had, gave such clear signs that he would also prefer to see Jake but not Sam, though with Steve I presumed it was because Jake no longer wore nappies and Sam did and of course, Sam also needed so much more supervision when out and about as well as having to take all the paraphernalia that goes with babies.

Jane left after about three hours and Jake happily waved her goodbye after being reassured that she would visit again, while Sam played contentedly on the floor with some toys and had no reaction to her leaving the room. But then, I had noticed Jane only said goodbye to Jake and hadn't even looked at Sam as she got up to go.

Shortly after Jane had gone and Jake had been tucked up in bed, Steve's mother phoned to see how her grandsons were, though once I had told her they were fine she started to push for information about what Jane and Steve were doing. I suggested due to confidentiality issues she should asked either Steve or her daughter Sharon what was going on in that corner and explained that I was not in a position to discuss what Jane was doing, but perhaps she could speak directly to her. Ooops…suddenly it felt like I had set off a firework with that comment as Steve's mother became quite angry, stating that the whole situation was down to 'that woman' and said it was quite probable that Jane was taking drugs because 'you just never know with people like that!'

Steve's mother definitely did not want her son and Jane getting back together, nor did she want either of them to have her grandsons in their care…trouble was, she didn't want the boys living with her or extended family members either. She appeared to just want them out of sight and out of mind irrespective of the effect this would have on her son, and on her grandchildren.

The last telephone call of the night was from Steve, who didn't sound as though he'd been drinking which was good. He asked if Jane was seeing the boys over the weekend and when told she wasn't he said he'd better see them then, though he also said he had nowhere to take them as Sharon was away for the weekend. I hadn't realised he'd been taking them to his sister's home when he had them and Jane obviously didn't know that either or she would have become quite angry. I decided I would forget the comment for now as it was February and the weather was so cold. The children needed to be somewhere warm to play and, if Sharon was allowing contact in her home I thought that maybe she would learn to have some feelings for these little boys and start to support Steve in his efforts to have them living with him permanently, as I didn't think the Department of Social Services would allow him to have them without the extra support that extended family members potentially can give.

Steve collected Jake and Sam at 10.00am the following morning, letting me know that he would be spending the day with them at a friend's home so they could stay warm and returned home with them mid-afternoon.

It was always a pleasure to see the children's reaction to their dad…big smiles and hugs all around.

They were freezing when they got home as it had been a bitter day and neither Steve nor I had realised that they would be spending most of the day Steve's car because his friend had gone out, and Steve hadn't thought to just call me to make sure I was in and ask if he could spend the time in our home with them instead.

Steve wasn't very happy with Jake and Sam either because they had messed up the inside of his car with the sweets, crisps and chips he had given them (what did he expect a baby and a toddler to do with food when they didn't have a table and plate?) Steve said they had driven around for over an hour before going to a park for Jake to run off some steam…he had then managed to find a pub with a children's room so they could all have a 'coke'…I hoped that was all Steve had drank. Still, they had got home safely enough and Steve didn't appear to have had a drink so I made hot drinks for everyone and we sat chatting as they all thawed out.

I explained to Steve that it must be hard for the children spending any length of time in the car and, with all his stuff still in there it was no wonder everything got messed up. I had thought he would have managed to un-pack most of his belongings since he was now, as far as we knew, living with a friend but he said there wasn't much space so he just got out what he needed for the day and put the stuff he wasn't using back into the car.

Steve complained that he didn't think anything had been sorted out when we had all met up with Phil the other day, saying that as he'd told Phil he wanted to have the children live with him, he had expected Phil to tell him to go rent a house for himself and the children and social services would then arrange for social security to pay the rent for him. To be honest, I'd also expected Phil to suggest that he rent a house and have an assessment but that option hadn't even been discussed at the meeting. Phil had appeared to have been more eager to get Jane feeling stronger in herself and having the children back with her than anything Steve had to say. Steve also felt that Jane's life was a 'bed of roses' at that time because she could do what she wanted without the hassle of looking after Jake and Sam while living in his house and taking all of his money…

Because Steve was so focused on the 'fun' that Jane was having (in his mind at least) we didn't get around to discussing any of the issues that directly related to him and what he was doing with his life before it was time for him to leave, though he did explain why he spent so much of his time in the pub…his explanation being that he didn't like to put anyone out so he stayed in the pub until late, returning to where he was staying just to go to sleep so he wasn't 'under anyone's feet' and…because of this he wasn't even getting to watch any television.

It would be a little while before we found out where Steve was actually staying…

Chapter 11

Steve had the children the following day, a Sunday, picking them up shortly after they had eaten lunch and returned them in time for their evening meal, stopping to chat for a little while and have a cup of coffee with us. Steve put his cigarettes on the coffee table as we talked and Jake picked up his box of matches. I told Jake to put the matches down and as Steve took them from him he looked at me and said 'I let him play with them, but I don't let Sam because he's too young'…Steve put the matches in his pocket while I sat almost speechless, though I did manage to say 'For goodness sake Steve …Jake is only two years old!'…Steve gave a sheepish grin, said his goodbyes and left, saying he would be back to pick Jake and Sam up toward the end of the week as he hoped to get some casual work done for a friend which would at least give him some money in his pocket.

That was one of the main problems for my family with this particular placement…everything was so random and it was left to Jane and Steve to decide when and if they were going to see their children. I could be getting ready to go out for the day and get a phone call because one of them had decided they wanted to see their children and then I would either have to negotiate a different time or cancel whatever I was doing in order to facilitate these parents…who appeared at times to have no idea that other people had lives to lead and things to be doing other than sitting at home waiting to be relieved of the 'chore' of looking after young children. I was looking forward to the day that a proper care plan was implemented and ground rules laid down for everyone to follow. This would then give Jake and Sam some sense of being settled rather than having no real routine apart from bedtime and early morning. It would also give our children guaranteed time out with everyone as a family rather than waiting for 'that phone call' just as we were going out and then having to be home in time for the little ones to be returned.

With a care plan it would also mean issues could be worked on because, although Steve appeared to be a loving dad and the children clearly enjoyed being with him, there were areas in the way he parented them that needed addressing, like his lack of understanding how dangerous some things, like matches, were in children's hands as the match incident had shown. Also I felt it would be appropriate for Phil to actually do some of the advising about child safety when out and about instead of always leaving it to me to point out when Steve had let himself and the children down by not being observant enough of their surroundings.

On reflection, it was lucky we didn't all carry a mobile phone in those days or our family could have had some very upsetting days out as I could have then been called back from whatever activity we were doing at the whim of Jane and Steve…

The following week I had Jake and Sam to myself for two whole days out of five. I got to spend a lovely Wednesday and Friday with them playing and doing normal things in and around our home. But with so little 'normal family time' together I wondered how on earth would I ever get them into any sort of routine. We had been expecting Jane to pick the boys up on the Monday at midday, just after they had eaten their lunch but, while Howard was out with them in the morning he had passed Jane in the town and she had looked away, though had said hello as they passed each other, she later phoned to explain she hadn't wanted to risk causing a scene in the street. I told her she had done the right thing…then she said she would be a little late collecting Jake and Sam but wasn't sure how late she would be. She was three hours late!

What I hadn't realised was that Jane had become friends with John, a male friend of ours who lived alone and was taking the children for their tea to his home, which was only a few houses away from us. We found this out when she returned with the boys two hours later and stopped for a chat once we had taken the children through their bedtime routine. Jane had chosen not to be a part of this activity, remaining in the lounge with Edward, James and Claire while Howard and I tucked her children into their beds for the night.

While we were all sitting together and our children had gone off to occupy themselves in the play room or their bedrooms, Jane started talking and seemed to be quite relaxed and totally confident in herself and of her feelings. Jane told us she had met John at the pub and asked if we knew him, something I'm sure she knew already because he was a neighbour of ours. I was quite concerned because John was fairly vulnerable at that time having only recently separated from his wife and we knew he was a total sucker for a sob story. Though Jane didn't say too much about John, she said enough for me to be quite concerned about how she would use him to get back at Steve. This left me in a difficult position as I would have to, at some time soon, diplomatically have a word with him.

Once again she was adamant that she didn't want Steve back in her life (for now?) and said she was planning on going abroad for a holiday with her sister. All she had to do was find somewhere for her daughters to stay while she was away. I kept quiet as I thought she was fishing for them to stay with us during the time she was abroad, and this was something, I'm sure that Phil would have agreed to had she asked him.

Jane talked about the time she had left Sam alone in the house in his cot, justifying her actions by saying she had told Steve that if he went out she was also going to go out and leave the baby at home…and that's what she had done. All she said she remembered of that time was finding herself quite a few miles away sitting on a bench and crying. Jane never clarified where the older three children were at this time even though I gently tried to coax it out of her as I didn't get the impression they were with her as she sat crying on that bench, but they weren't in the house either. We talked about how dangerous it was to leave small children alone in a house and how even little ones that were in a cot could have accidents if not checked on periodically. She didn't know for how long Steve would be away from the house that she was leaving a baby in, who may have needed feeding and changing and, an even worse scenario would have been, if she had thought that Steve was going to be home soon after she went out…and Steve didn't know she had actually carried out her threat and had left the baby alone. They may both have been away from him for hours…even overnight. I asked her if she had even thought of the possibility that they may both have been involved in separate accidents, and that child could then have been alone for days. I hadn't intended to lay a guilt trip on her, but she had to know that she couldn't just walk out on her children in the future and presume they would be okay, or that someone else would just take over the caring of them, especially if no-one knew they were home alone.

Jane left long after Jake and Sam had settled to sleep for the night, but said she would have the children for the whole of the following day, which she did, picking them up at 09.45am and letting me collect them at 4.30pm…when she explained the large bruise which was under Sam's eye by saying he had fallen off the bed while playing. I couldn't understand how anyone could allow a small baby to be playing upstairs in a bedroom with no adult supervision, again I was left wondering how much time she actually spent with Jake and Sam when she had them for her contact. I let Phil know about the bruise and his response was that 'kids will be kids'…I wondered what he would have said had this happened during Steve's contact time? Probably that I'd have to get Sam over to the hospital for x-rays and have it properly documented to possibly be used in evidence at some future date. I documented it anyway as I did with all events, good and bad.

On the Thursday Steve had the boys for a few hours and took them to the park to play, returning them in time for a quick meal and bed. Due to the time they returned, they missed out on the bath time fun so it wasn't until the Friday morning that I noticed a faint bruise on Sam's tummy, about two inches above his belly button, and what appeared to be a cigarette burn on Jake's thigh. I spoke to Phil about this and made an appointment for both Jake and Sam to see the doctor. When I had asked Jake how he hurt his leg he told me it happened when he was at his mum's house and she had a cigarette, but told the doctor that his daddy did it with a cigarette. We had one quite confused little boy who couldn't or wouldn't tell us who did it, but clearly knew what the mark was.

Steve had made arrangements to have the boys on both the Saturday and Sunday of that week and, as there was confusion over who may have caused the injuries to them during the week, Phil agreed that this contact should go ahead. Sometimes it just seemed like social workers either didn't want the hassle of 'troublesome placements' or just wanted to give their clients enough rope to hang themselves and then they could move forward quicker with the cases they were working on. I think Phil was hoping that Steve would make a major mistake and then be written out of the picture, so to speak, and more effort could then be put into helping Jane care for the children. However, though we had concerns about Steve, he hadn't actually stood back from being a very hands-on father while in our home as we had witnessed him changing nappies and giving cuddles as well as playing rough and tumble with Jake. Sometimes, while watching Steve playing with Jake and Sam you could see how easily the children could get the odd bruise and carry on giggling away without noticing they had been hurt. Most children get the odd bruise when having fun, not when being abused. Steve had also helped on one occasion with the bedtime routine, so our view of how things were progressing was slightly different from that of social services.

When Steve arrived to pick the boys up I asked him about the bruise to Sam's tummy and about the cigarette burn on Jake's leg, explaining that I'd had to take them to the doctor the day before to have it all recorded. Steve told me he had noticed a mark on Jake's leg when he had taken him to the toilets in the park, but as it was dimly lit he had thought it was just a spot and had forgotten about it by the time they got home. Steve had asked Jake how it happened but I hadn't heard what Jake had told him, but Steve told me that he didn't think Jane would deliberately hurt the boys so it must have been an accident and she was probably too scared to say anything in case she got into trouble for it.

I don't know if Steve was trying to provoke an argument or not, but he then said that if it had happened when Jake and Sam had been with Jane on Tuesday, the last day she had seen them, it must mean that we were not looking after his children properly to have not noticed it for a couple of days. He didn't appear to ponder the possibility that he may have been considered as capable of causing the marks himself...just that we hadn't bathed the children or we would have seen it before he did the day before. Although there really was no reason to, because I didn't have to justify anything to him, he was the client, not me, I explained that with the exception of the Tuesday, when they returned too tired for a bath, they bathed every evening and had clean clothes on every day, sometimes twice a day, and they had three meals a day when they were with us and a packed lunch most days they were with him because I provided it for them. At that time I was also making up a packed lunch for Steve so that he could have a picnic with the children. I did this because I think children learn better table manners quicker when eating with adults, as well as to give Steve something to eat because he was just so very thin and hungry looking.

Following this conversation Steve took Jake and Sam out for the day, returning them in time for their tea, but he didn't stop himself longer than a few minutes to reassure us there were no fresh injuries on the children from that day

He picked the children up after breakfast the following day and returned them early evening again. This time he stayed and got involved with the bedtime routine and gave Jake and Sam their baths, after which he told us that Jake had said he burned his leg with a cigarette while at Jane's house and it had happened on the Monday. Steve told us that as

Jake got out of the bath he pointed to his leg and said 'look at that! Mum did it with a cigarette in the bedroom'...His words or Steve's, I didn't know, but it would be logged.

Later that evening, Jane's sister telephoned to let us know Jane was too poorly to see the children at the moment but didn't go into any details about how ill or what was wrong, simply said that they would be in touch soon to sort out seeing Jake and Sam...it would be three days before we heard from her and she saw Jake again.

Two days later Steve took Jake and Sam out for the day, returning with them after tea and staying to help bathe them both and settle them into bed. Once they were settled we had a coffee and Steve told me that though Phil had told him he mustn't question Jake about the burn to his leg, it was gnawing at him and he just needed to know who had done it and when. He told me Jake had told him it was his mum. I reminded him that we already knew this and it was best if he didn't discuss it any more with Jake as he was only a very little man and we didn't want him fixating on it or picking at it. Steve then told me that Jane had a new boyfriend...this he had found out from Jake.

What he hadn't found out was that her new 'boyfriend' was our friend John, and what Jane didn't know was that John had told me they were just friends and he didn't want to get involved but she just kept turning up on his doorstep asking to go in and then wouldn't leave for hours. One evening she had arrived and fallen asleep on his settee and slept for several hours before waking and going home.

John had come to me before I'd had the chance to pop over to see him and ask about the relationship between him and Jane because he felt concerned that she was a very needy person, but was sensible enough to realise that he was very needy as well. He told me that he couldn't cope with a relationship at that time but Jane just kept arriving and he didn't know how to tell her not to. He wished he'd never been in the pub the night they had met and was full of regrets about giving her his address, not realising she would ever just arrive like she had. He was after advice about how to get out of the situation he was in which I tried to give but, due to the confidentiality of fostering I really couldn't tell him anything I knew about Jane. All I could do was advise him not to open the door if it was her and of course, warn him that she may be using him to get back at Steve.

Even giving John the little warning was a bit dodgy because had Jane arrived at his home and he told her anything I'd said, she could have reported me for even mentioning Steve and I may have been in trouble with the social services. It's a very fine line you have to tread when working with vulnerable children and adults.

It is always so sad that children are used not only as weapons by warring parents but also as spies for them. With a child as young as Jake nothing is secret, as they tend to be natural chatterboxes at times and have no sense of whether they are repeating something secret or not because they haven't learnt the basics of secrets and lies. That comes a little later in their life, so Jake had just chatted away about the last time he was at his mums and out popped a name that Steve didn't know, so he had then questioned Jake about this man and got all the answers he wanted, though they were not the answers he had wanted to hear. I told Steve that it was best to not discuss anything the boys did at Jane's if possible and certainly not to question Jake about who was at the house when the children were there because Jake may then clam up and not tell us important things that the social worker may need to know about.

He listened and nodded, but I knew he would continue to question Jake now that Jane had someone else in her life. I couldn't tell Steve that actually the man in her life was our friend either because I didn't want him to go knocking on John's door...I did however tell him that not everything may be as clear cut as Jake made it sound when chatting in the way children do.

The following day Jane phoned early and asked if she could just have Jake for the day so, while Sam had his morning sleep she popped round and quickly left with Jake in tow, returning with him well after his bedtime. She didn't come into our home, just quickly explained the bump above Jakes eye was caused when he had jammed a box on his head and said goodbye to him at the door. As she walked away Jane called back that if Steve wanted the boys for the following weekend that was fine with her...and with that she was gone. For fourteen weeks we had no contact from her whatsoever.

Chapter 12

Steve telephoned later that evening, he sounded slightly drunk and quite annoyed. He didn't want to discuss Jake and Sam, just to complain that Jane's' boyfriend was at his house. He told me that they were supposed to be having three months living apart to sort out the mess that was their life, and what had Jane done? Not only moved on to another man but let him move in! I reminded him as gently as I could that it had been his choice to move out of the family home and that not everything was as it may seem, but he just slurred that he loved her and had just needed some time, for what he didn't say...though he did say he was gutted before hanging up.

I knew John hadn't moved in with Jane so knew that if she had moved someone else in at least it wasn't him.

This was the first night that Jake screamed out as he had a nightmare, and screamed until Howard got to him and calmed him down. He couldn't say what had scared him so much but at least he slept soundly through the night after he had been calmed.

Early in the morning Steve telephoned to say he wanted to have the children for the day and when he came to pick them up said he had been to his house the night before and seen Jane's boyfriend there, as he then complained that Jane had seen only Jake the day before I knew he must have been in the house and talking with her. He clearly didn't want to discuss things with me and promptly left with his children, returning just after midday because Jake had become distressed and he didn't know what to do with a child who was fast approaching three years of age that couldn't or wouldn't tell him what the problem was. The only thing was, Steve didn't want to leave the children yet so stayed for a coffee and another chat while the children played quietly and said he hoped that once Jake had calmed down he could take them out again for the afternoon.

I liked talking with Steve because he seemed totally unguarded about what he said. Sometimes he would say things that meant we would have an in depth conversation about childcare and safety, and also things that I'd advise him I would have to let Phil know about, but this was all good as he tended to take on board things I suggested to him and accepted that there were things he may say that would have to go further, whether they reflected badly on him or Jane, I couldn't take sides when the children's futures were the issue.

Once the children were settled and Jake had calmed down I walked with them and Steve to his car, it was filthy and absolutely stank of chips, with sticky sweets and bits of fried potato all over the back seat. No wonder the children were so bloody filthy today following their outing with Steve, but I helped strap them into their grubby seats, wearing their second outfit of the day and smiled as I waved them off for an afternoon of fun in the park, Steve hadn't smelt of alcohol and was talking quite normally so I knew he hadn't been to the pub. He said he'd been to a park this morning and was now off to another park for the afternoon so I just thought for a dad, Steve certainly seemed to enjoy playing in parks with his children. It didn't enter my mind that he had nowhere else to take them as I believed that he was now back staying with his sister and spent the days there when he had them.

For the following three days Steve had his children for the whole day as Jane's sister telephoned again and said she was still too poorly to see them. One morning, when he arrived to pick them up, he chose to wait and play indoors with Jake rather than wake Sam from his morning sleep, or just take Jake out on his own and he also helped on two of the evenings with their bedtime routine. On the night he didn't stay and help, while the children were having their bath, Jake got very excited and while laughing kept asking Sam to grab his willy. I asked him if anyone else touched him there and his said his mummy did. I made a note of this and reported it to Phil, not that I was overly concerned, just that it was something that needed to be recorded in case he made any further comments or started acting out in any other way that may have suggested further investigation was needed.

On the third day, Steve told me he had been called to the local wine bar the previous evening because he was known there. The manager had telephoned him because Jane was there, drunk but on her own. Steve said that when he got there Jane told him that she was getting married to her boyfriend and that while he was there, Jane's sister had arrived with one of Jane's daughters from her first marriage and just left the child with them. Steve said he tried to get Jane to go home and stop showing herself up in public but that he ended up leaving them both in the wine bar around 29pm when he went home because he didn't know what else to do. I didn't say anything to Steve but spoke to Phil later to give him a quick update because as far as I knew Jane was supposed to be too ill to see her sons so should be too ill for visiting wine bars and certainly shouldn't be in them with a young daughter while she herself was drunk.

The following day the children were with me all day; this was two days after the bath time incident with Jake asking Sam to pull his willy. That evening he got all excited in the bath again, this time saying that when mummy squeezed it and it felt nice and she said it would be all right. Jake also said Sam liked it when their mummy squeezed his willy as well.

I was a little more concerned now so made another note and let Phil know what had been said first thing in the morning.

The next day was Saturday and Steve had arranged to have the children for the day. He arrived in the morning and was in a dreadful state. He could hardly stand, had a split lip and black eye and was holding onto his ribs. According to him, Jane's boyfriend and his brothers had attacked him the night before and beaten him up. He agreed that it was a bit stupid of him to have gone to the house in the first place, especially as he had been drinking but gave a sheepish smile, a painful shrug and said 'that's life isn't it?'

Due to how battered and in pain he looked I suggested leaving the children for the day and popping to the hospital instead but Steve was insistent that he spend time with the children and wanted to take them out. I finally managed to convince Steve to take just Jake, as at least he wouldn't then need the pushchair, nor would he have a child who required picking up periodically and nappy changes, though I hadn't been happy that either child had seen him in such a state.

It was just on tea time when Steve's sister Sharon turned up with Jake and explained that Steve was at the hospital waiting to see a doctor and have x-rays done. Sharon didn't stop and once she had gone Jake asked if his mum was going to visit the following day. When I'd asked him if he wanted her to he gave a very definite and emphatic 'No' in response and went to the playroom to rummage through the toys.

It was four weeks before Steve was well enough to drive to our home and visit Jake and Sam following the assault by Jane's boyfriend and his brothers, and though I know he was encouraged to press charges he didn't; probably because he felt it was partly his own fault and of course, whatever he had done to cause the new boyfriend to get so angry would also then come out. Steve kept his own counsel about that night and didn't speak with me about the incident during any of the daily telephone calls he made over that period.

I was a little surprised that during this time Sharon hadn't once offered to drop Steve off to our home so he could spend time with Jake and Sam, but at least she was looking after Steve so we just made the most of the time we had to be like any other family.

I have to be honest and say that the time when we were just left to get on with our lives with no interruptions from Steve and Jane was lovely. We couldn't plan very much as we never knew if Steve was suddenly going to call to say he wanted to visit the next day. We had seen Jane around and every time she had noticed us she had either popped into a shop or turned her head away…clearly indicating she didn't want to see Jake and Sam or talk to us. Our weekends especially were wonderful as the whole family could do what they pleased, whenever they pleased, without either Howard or me telling Edward, James and Claire that we had to be home at certain times for Jake and Sam to be collected or dropped off…so although our kids were at school and following term time routines, it felt like we were on holiday.

Just before Steve started seeing the children again we heard a noise outside just after midnight but on looking outside we didn't see anyone so presumed it must have been an animal. Unfortunately, the next morning we found the passenger side tyres on our car had both been deflated. This could have been a total random act, but over the years since this incident, when working with some of our more 'problematic' families, we have had various tyres let down and attempts to get into our home that haven't happened when working the easier (not that any placement is easy) placements. This is just another thing foster carers have to consider when going into this line of work...social services do give the address of foster carers to birth parents because they may be having contact within the fostering home...and sometimes, as in the case of Mia[*], it is accidently provided to the birth family because paperwork is sent out that hasn't had the foster carers address removed from it.

---

[*] Mia by Lizzie Scott

Chapter 13

The first time Steve saw Jake and Sam following the assault he took them to the park. Both children became so excited at seeing their dad after just hearing him speak to them over the telephone for so many weeks.

It was lovely to see them pounce on him as he came into our home. Sam was now much sturdier on his legs as he was spending so much time walking around in the house and garden. He had also started to walk a little more while we were out if we weren't in any hurry to get somewhere. Unfortunately though, while at the park both children had accidents, Sam fell off a roundabout and had a huge graze from his cheek to his forehead and Jake had a large graze on his arm and one on his thigh from falling from a swing. Luckily Steve had managed to calm them when the accidents happened and they came home showing off their war wounds. Even so, these injuries had to be logged and reported to Phil, as foster carers could not be held above suspicion if children sustained injuries while in their care.

Two days later poor Jake went down with chicken pox so Steve stayed at our home daily for the following week when he saw the children. During this time he took over all of the care for the children, even using the kitchen to prepare their lunch and get them their drinks and supervised the bedtime routine if he was still around. This period gave me plenty of time not only to observe Steve with his children but to talk about what was going on in his life. He told me he had managed to get part-time work in a bar during the evenings as he needed to be around during the days to spend time with Jake and Sam, if he was to be considered in the long term for having them live with him. He told me he had upset his family by going against their wishes for the children to be adopted, and though he wasn't pleased with his parents and sister for pushing him to walk away from the boys, he seemed to understand their concerns, it was just that he wasn't ready to walk away and said he never would be.

Steve was certainly proving to be a very committed father to Jake and Sam and, while in our home he appeared to be quite observant to what they were doing, taking time to make sure they were safe and happy and learning Sam's routine with sleep times. This was something I hoped he would be able to continue once he started taking them out again…but of course, while sitting comfortably and just chatting over a slow cup of coffee, you are not always so guarded about the things you say, and Steve let slip that he was living in his car. That explained why it was always such a mess and he always looked quite crumpled. He didn't say how long he had lived like that and said he had friends that let him use their bathrooms and there was always the toilets in parks to have a quick clean up…he also used the restrooms in the wine bar where he worked to wash and change. Steve said he spent some of his contact days in launderettes as well, trying to make these the days when it rained and they couldn't go to the park.

I realised then the commitment Steve had for his children. He had given up full-time employment to be able to fulfil the social services need for him to see his children and spend as much time as possible with them. I also realised that there would be no way for Steve to manage any sort of routine with the boys until he had a proper roof over his head and he had no chance of getting that roof while he was officially unemployed and definitely of no fixed abode. He had little money as he was only working a few evenings a week so wouldn't be able to afford private rent and while the children lived with us the local authority wouldn't give him a house. This was quite a mess and a huge obstacle to overcome.

But of course, Steve's biggest obstacle was Phil, who appeared to have little to zero confidence in him whatsoever.

In the evening of the first day Steve had managed to take them out once Jake had stopped being infectious, while getting ready for bed, Jake suddenly started shouting 'Mums a fucking fucker! She's fucking fucking!' as he swung his arms in the air as if to thump himself in the face. I was quite shocked by his language and told him not to say such things as it was rude and not nice words to say…Jake quietened, sulked a little and settled to sleep.

The following day was the first time I was aware that Steve was annoyed with me following his contact with Jake and Sam. Not because of anything he had said, simply because he looked annoyed and left as soon as the children were through the front door. Jake told me that they had been looking for me earlier because I hadn't been home when they arrived. Because he asked where I'd been I explained that I had to go out sometimes and hadn't been expecting them home early in the day or I would have been waiting for them. He said they'd gone to the pub for the day and gone back there because I was out. I would have to talk to Steve about taking the children to the pub for a whole day as it wasn't the place for children to be for long periods of time.

Two days later Steve asked if I could prepare a packed lunch for Jake and Sam as he was taking them to a park that was nowhere near any shops. As I now knew he had little money I packed a lunch for him as well, just as I had in the earlier days of this placement. Steve also asked for a change of clothes and their pyjamas. They returned later than expected and were absolutely filthy, though they were in their pyjamas and Steve said they were ready for bed. Once he had left, the children had to have a bath and some food as Jake told us he hadn't had any tea.

Steve had arranged with his parents to visit them the following day and stay for the weekend. Steve was due to pick the children up at 10.00am. He telephoned at 1100am to say he was running late and we had a few words as I'd had an appointment which then had to be cancelled. He finally arrived at midday...returning an hour later as he had forgotten something and the children wanted a drink. He really didn't look very well, though I suppose if you are sleeping in your car it is to be expected. While we all had a drink Sharon telephoned and told me that the situation was not working and that Steve should not continue to see the boys on a daily basis.

This woman was quite a forceful person and insistent in her opinion. Sharon wasn't happy when I told her that what he needed right then was her support and that she should be talking to Steve about her ideas instead of to me. I passed the telephone to Steve; after a few words were spoken he sighed and put the phone down. Apparently after Steve had made all the arrangements to take Jake and Sam to visit their grandparents for the weekend, Sharon had telephoned them and convinced them to change their mind, she had just told Steve it was now not convenient for them to visit. Steve asked if he could make a call to his parents from our home, which he did. I don't know what was said during the conversation but when Steve replaced the receiver he looked a lot brighter and the planned visit went ahead.

I gathered from Steve that the reason he had been late arriving was because his sister had been trying to make him walk away from Jake and Sam. She had told him that taking them to visit their grandparents was wrong because they would be building relationships with people that would play no part in their future. Steve was quite clear that he wanted to have the children live with him at some time in the near future and was willing to do whatever it took to make that a reality. He had given up his day job because he'd been told he needed to prove to the social services that he was committed to them...but there was no help in return with any sort of funding for when he spent time, almost daily, out with them. There was also no support from Phil regarding getting somewhere that Steve and the boys could live. Poor Steve, he did seem to be trying to do his best but this just didn't please many people at all…though mostly it didn't appear to please his sister.

Chapter 14

It had been discussed with Phil that there was a possibility for Steve to move with Jake and Sam into a residential unit so he could have a full assessment made of him as a single parent caring for his children on a full time basis.

These units can be quite invasive as they consist of small two bedroom apartments with a lounge diner, kitchen and bathroom with (so we were told) cameras in all the rooms to ensure the children's safety. Phil wanted to know that Steve would manage not only the day to day living but also had the commitment needed to spend every night caring as well. We were all waiting for this to be formalised and set in place when Steve had gone to stay with the children at his parents for the weekend. While he was still there his mother telephoned to say that she felt it would be in everyone's best interest if the plan didn't materialise. She thought the best long term plan would be for Jake and Sam to be adopted. His mother and sister would never give any reasons for their thinking adoption would be the right way to move forward…just that it was the right thing to do.

We obviously hadn't known Steve for as long as his family had but, from what we saw, not physically regarding looks as Steve was usually quite scruffy, but what can you expect if someone is living out of a car, but of the commitment he was giving and the way he played with the children, we could see no reason why he couldn't at least be given the chance to prove his family wrong, or prove them right, but all his family seemed to be doing was trying to get me to press Phil to move ahead with an adoption. Out of sight, out of mind may have been okay for them, but I knew it would break Steve to lose his children after he had given up so much for them. Also, I didn't think it was right to be talking about these things if the children were around, as Jake was old enough to pick up the general gist of a conversation and could get upset if he thought they were trying to get rid of him.

Chapter 15

On the Friday, after Steve had left with Jake and Sam I received a telephone call from Alison, one of my favourite social workers in our local area office. She wanted to know if I would be on standby for this weekend as there was a mother about to give birth and as soon as the baby was born it would need to be removed from the hospital.

There would be no following the six hour protocol with this delivery. She knew all about Jake and Sam but also knew we all loved working with new babies. Sue explained that this would be a very short term placement (oh the times we heard that) as both of the parents had major mental health issues and would never be able to parent their child. I agreed to the placement and was then told I had to get to the hospital for a meeting with everyone involved in this placement within the hour!

I arrived at the maternity unit, where the meeting was being held. As I walked in a large man approached me and asked who I was. I must have looked a bit surprised as people come and go all the time in the reception area of the hospital without being asked who they were, so he asked me if my name was Lorraine. Ok, so he knew who I was, but who was he? This burly man looked around and then gave me instructions on where the meeting was being held and told me to answer anyone who questioned me on the way.

As I walked through a set of double doors there were two more men standing there who asked for my name, which I gave. They also directed me to the meeting room which was crowded with social workers from the adult mental health care team as well as the child care team. There were also representatives from the police, mental health doctors and someone from the maternity unit. The meeting was a brief one but full information was shared with everyone who would be involved with this placement from that moment on.

The parents had had a baby some years before, that had been placed for adoption and that was the plan for this baby. I wasn't made aware of any efforts that may have been made to help this couple keep their first baby or if, sadly, they were just too high risk due to their mental health issues to even have been allowed to try a family unit. All I knew of that first baby was that he had been adopted quite soon after his delivery.

The parents lived in rented accommodation which they had cleared of everything…there was nothing in the kitchen, not even the sink and nothing in any of the other rooms either. There wasn't even a bed as they considered themselves to be 'minimalists' so just slept on the floor on some blankets, eating their main meal daily at the Mental Health Unit of their local hospital. The only room that had anything in was the one that was made like a shrine to their first child, so *everyone* knew this would be a very painful and upsetting experience for these parents, more so than for most of the parents I had worked with so far, because these parents couldn't do anything to change their circumstances no matter what support was put in place to help them.

Due to the severity of both parents mental health issues the baby was considered to be at high risk of abduction for as long as it remained within the hospital grounds, so the hospital would telephone me as soon as the delivery was over and I would then need to get to the hospital as fast as possible following that call.

There was also, of course, the possible risk to other mothers and their babies who were in the maternity unit at that time, as the parents could get very violent and threatening once the delivery had actually taken place.

Every precaution was put in place to protect not only this baby and other patients, but also the parents from their own actions, which would be beyond their control.

It was all so very sad yet so necessary.

Once everything was agreed and the plan formalised I was shown out of the meeting by a policeman who checked all the corridors were still clear and went home, where I got busy preparing the crib and washing out the new baby clothes I already had as well as popping out to purchase some of the paraphernalia that is needed when a new born baby comes home.

Where normally I would be so excited about having a new baby in our home, this time that excitement was tinged with a sorrow I hadn't felt before. The parents I usually worked with when new babies were involved had a history of abuse towards children. These didn't, they just had a terrible mental illness.

It was all so very, very sad.

Of course, what I didn't consider at this time was how long it may take to find an adoptive family for a baby with possible complex future needs. To me a baby was simply, well, a baby...something small that needs lots of cuddles between putting food in one end and clearing up the mess at the other end.

It didn't enter my mind at this stage of our fostering career that there could be any delay other than those created through the clients, their solicitors or social workers wishes for assessments...it had been made perfectly clear that there would be no delay on any level with this child moving to its forever family...

But of course, mental health concerns, in fact any medical concern, creates its own delay as assessments have to be carried out on the child to see how much of a risk the child is at of developing symptoms or illness later in life and these assessments can't even begin until the baby is old enough to respond to simple instructions.

Nathan would actually spend six months with our family before meeting his wonderful new mum, dad and big sister.

I had the telephone call in the early hours of the Saturday morning to let me know that a baby boy had been safely delivered and telling me where to go to pick him up.

The concerns were so high for the safety of this child that once born he had been taken from the delivery room once weighed straight to the children's ward. If the parents went looking for him among the new babies on the postnatal wards they wouldn't find him. His birth notes were placed under his mattress instead of at the end of the cot and he had also been wrapped in a pink blanket so anyone would think he was a baby girl. I was advised to arrive at the hospital ward for 08.30am, by which time the doctor would have arrived to discharge him and that I was to get him dressed and to be out of the hospital as quickly as possible, before most of the patients were even through having their breakfasts.

I got to the hospital having left Howard with our very excited children. They were looking forward to having a new born baby in our home as it meant they all got to give cuddles to him, unlike with the older children who didn't always want to be hugged, though then they had the fun of playing with kids toys if they wanted to without having anyone laugh at them…definite benefits to having little brothers and sisters!

I must have looked, to some people, quite conspicuous as I arrived because, though I didn't want to draw attention to myself, I was aware that there were a few people around and here I was heading into the ward with a baby bag and it wasn't even visiting time. I had been lucky enough to have been told not to take a baby car seat into the hospital as this could have hampered the speed with which I could leave the ward...nonetheless, I was laden with my handbag and the baby bag containing some clothes and a shawl going in, and the bag full of the baby's milk and items his parents had insisted on having for him when rushing out...and the baby in my arms...and no escort.

Everyone had considered it a safer option for me to be alone as it would draw less attention to us, because it was only when leaving the maternity unit that you had an escort with the nurse carrying the baby...I almost ran from that hospital. I had no idea what the parents looked like and, though I knew the mother was still somewhere inside, the father could be anyone and anywhere.

Where I had looked over my shoulder as I went into the building, I only checked the corridor as I left the ward and, because there was no-one in sight just rushed out of the building as fast as my legs could carry me. When I got to my car I strapped the baby into the seat while trying to check all around me that no-one was watching and then, having a last check that the car park was clear and that no-one appeared to be watching me I jumped into the car, locked the doors and drove out of the car park quickly, heading in the opposite direction to where we lived.

If anyone was following, I was not going to lead them straight to my home.

I did quite a detour around the local estates near the hospital and popped through a couple of small villages on the way home and once satisfied I truly wasn't being followed by anyone, I turned the car toward home ready for a nice cup of coffee and to introduce the latest member of our family to Howard and our children.

Alison had also been telephoned by the hospital staff so was aware that I had been to pick the baby up. Shortly after I got home she called to discuss the placement further. I was told that due to the nature of the parent's mental health it was vital that no-one other than her and other professionals directly involved with this placement knew who was caring for him and where he was living.

I was to register him with our doctor under his birth name, which is the only legal thing to do, but that it had to be recorded that he was known as something else when having his postnatal appointments. Under no circumstances could they call out his real name, they had to use another name…He would be known as whatever we wanted him to be known as.

This was something new to me and in all the years we fostered it was the only time our children got to name a child that shared our home. They chatted excitedly about their new baby 'brother' and decided they would like him to be called Nathan and he shared our surname for all appointments with medical professionals and health visitors.

As far as all our friends knew, Nathan had been placed with us from a different local authority which was some miles from where we lived because they had no available foster carers who wanted to take such little ones.

Only one person other than us knew his background, but even she didn't know his given name…my dear friend and fellow foster carer Elizabeth. We shared everything!

So Nathan was settled into our family over the three day weekend that Jake, Sam and Steve were away and due to the nature of the placement we were expecting that he would be settled with his new family within a couple of months at the most.

There would be no delay in placing him as there would be no parenting assessment to consider. All that needed to be done was for the Department of Social Services to find a family that would accept this beautiful baby with an unknown future ahead of him. Would he inherit a mental illness? No-one knew, but it was less likely that he would suffer as his parents did if he didn't grow up in an environment where he could learn at least some, if not all of their behaviours.

Chapter 16

Jake and Sam were not happy to see our new arrival in the crib and they didn't want to say goodnight to Steve when they got home on the Monday evening, but settled to sleep once he had gone and they had both had a little cuddle and poke at Nathan. They slept soundly all night and did not wake until almost 9.00am the following day. Luckily James and Claire had been taken to school by a friend who knew we'd had a new placement over the weekend, so although Nathan had woken early for his feed it meant I didn't have to wake the boys.

Something must have gone very well over the weekend, as when I had Sam on my lap getting him dressed he suddenly looked at me and spontaneously landed a great big kiss on my cheek. Up until then they had both only given kisses at bedtime, but he looked so very happy at that moment…maybe it was because he knew I was getting him ready to go out with his daddy and the thought just made him happy. I'll never know, but it was a step forward for this little boy who had been such a quiet little lad who tended to play nicely with toys and just watch the world around him while not always appearing to be a part of it, or even wanting to be a part of it.

This was another sad thing we had noticed about children who travel through the care system. Some had an amazing ability to just sit on the side-lines of life and observe, almost as though they don't think they deserve to be a part of whatever is going on around them.

Steve took the children out on the Tuesday and the Wednesday to the park. Almost every time he took them out they went to a park in or around the village we lived in. On the Tuesday Steve had returned with the children just as I was going to meet James and Claire from school. Jake and Sam had been so filthy I'd had to ask Steve to take them out for an extra half hour as there was no way I would be seen out with two little urchins that looked like they hadn't seen water in a month!

Although we were happy to bend a few rules and allow Steve to use our bathroom so he could shower in the early days when he had nowhere to live; and we were happy to provide him with picnic meals because he had very little money…we were nowhere near feeling at ease to leave him alone in our home with the children. That would not only have bent a few rules…that would have completely broken them.

When he returned he bathed both boys and got them ready for their beds before tea, then stopped and joined them for a meal. This was something new for Jake and Sam as they hadn't sat at the table with their dad for a meal since they had arrived. They had eaten either in the park or in the car depending on the weather. This went down so well with the three of them that it happened quite a few times after that during the rest of the placement. Of course…I think this would have been considered as 'breaking the rules' somewhat more than we had already done over the past few months as it slightly blurred the boundaries of social services plans, foster carers and clients, but I just considered it as 'bending the rules' a little bit and showing the children a clear message that their dad was welcome in our home and that we were working together so they could all share their own home one day.

Chapter 17

On the Thursday morning Jake woke and complained of a pain in his right foot. Every time he put his foot down he cried out in pain. When I looked I noticed faint bruising and it looked a little swollen. Jake had seemed okay when he had come home the day before but clearly wasn't okay now. I asked Jake if he knew why it hurt and he said that his daddy did it with stones when they were playing. I asked again and he told me that when he was playing with his dad, his dad was throwing stones at him...and that's when he thought it had happened.

I telephoned Steve to explain that if he wanted to see the children that day he would need to take Jake to the hospital because his foot was giving him a lot of pain and looked to be a bit swollen, or he could wait until I returned after taking him. Steve just mumbled that Jake must have done something the day before and, because he hadn't used his foot all night that was why the pain had come out that morning, and that of course he would take him to the hospital before going to the park. I didn't tell him what Jake had told me.

When Steve arrived to pick Jake and Sam up he told me that Jake had been mucking around in the car and somehow got his foot caught under the handbrake and thought that may be how it had happened. They returned that evening having been to the hospital, with Jake's foot and ankle bandaged and the message that if things hadn't improved within three days he was to go back to hospital for further investigation. Steve didn't elaborate on anything else that the hospital had said or mention any other possible cause for the swelling.

Over the next five days you couldn't fault Steve in his care of Jake and Sam. When he was in our home, which was now for a couple of hours a day due to the weather, he was attentive and affectionate. The fact that Steve was spending so much time in our home when he had care of his sons was something else I couldn't tell Phil, because as far as he was concerned Steve had to prove how good he was by taking the boys to his own home and caring for them without my support.

Steve had told me that he was now sharing a friends flat and couldn't take Jake and Sam there during the day because his friend worked nights and needed to sleep during the day, so he would sit quietly in our home and read to the children, play rough and tumble or just sit and watch children's programmes with them. He stayed for quite a few meals with just Jake and Sam, happily using our kitchen to prepare whatever I had purchased for the day and then joined our family for Sunday lunch…though he had to promise not to mention anything to Phil as I didn't think that would go down too well with social services…he was after all a 'client' and one that was fighting for his children while everyone else was appearing to be trying to take them away from him. I could understand the departments concerns regarding Steve and his children, but we found a certain simple honesty about him. What you saw was what you got, and Steve was a very sad dad trying to do what was right by his children and trying not to annoy a social worker who had ultimate control of where this case was going. A tricky place for anyone to be in, made worse for Steve because he didn't appear to belong anywhere.

Because I was reporting back to Phil about how well things were going he had agreed that Steve could take the boys away for a week. This was great on several levels because it meant the children had a holiday with their dad and extended family, we had a week to be with our children, and I had extra daytime hours to get to know Nathan better and get a routine sorted that would make life easier to cater for all the age groups living in our home…as well as cater to Steve's needs, which though simple, took up quite a bit of my time as he spent so many hours a week in our home.

Phil was still appearing to be very much focused on them returning to live with their mother, who hadn't seen them or been in touch with me or Phil to even ask after them for some time…but Phil was a ladies man so I guess he was just biding his time and waiting for Jane to be 'strong enough' to come back into the arena and care for her sons.

The problem was, the children shouldn't have been just left dangling in the care system. They deserved better than that and, while we were happy to have them share our home, they had a dad who was willing to be assessed, a dad who wanted to be assessed, a dad who wanted to be the main care for them and would do whatever was asked of him…except walk away. Also, while Jake and Sam were sharing our home it meant that another little family who needed care couldn't. Not that we ever wanted to rush a child or family out, we just didn't want things to be left dragging slowly through the system as this was the children's lives and they deserved better. They deserved to be settled where they were going to stay and Steve deserved to be assessed as capable or not of looking after his sons.

Because Phil was so focused on the children returning to live with their mother, I sometimes felt a little sorry when I had to phone him up to let him know that one or both of the children had come home having had an accident while out for the day with their dad, because though I know children can fall and be okay, every incident that resulted in an injury had to be reported back. If I hadn't reported these incidents and Jane had suddenly come back on the scene she could well accuse me of harming the children and then I could be in a lot of trouble. There is also a very fine line between working with a parent towards the return of their children and colluding with them to get the end result that they want, which may not be in the child's best interest, so in some ways we were walking quite a tightrope with this placement because we were supporting Steve in his endeavours to get his children back and sometimes, quite a few times actually, we were definitely bending the rules somewhat.

The main thing we had to focus on was, irrespective of what the relationship between father and sons looked like…was if the children were actually going to be safe if cared for fulltime by their dad.

It was with a heavy heart that I telephoned Phil to let him know that although the children returned home looking happy and well fed after Steve had taken them away for a whole week, Sam had a two inch graze and huge bruise on his face having fallen into the corner of a room and a pale bruise to his eye. Phil said he'd had misgivings about Steve's abilities to care appropriately for the children all along and that he shouldn't have been swayed by positive arguments from me and Howard and of course Steve, who had even managed to scrape together the monies needed to take them on a little holiday.

Two days later I had to telephone him again after bathing the children because I noticed a fingertip type bruise on Jake's spine along with grazing and bruising on his shoulder following contact with Steve.

Chapter 18

Due to the amount of bruises and grazes that the children had I was advised that Steve could no longer supervise bathing and undressing alone. He was so good with the children that if he'd arrived early in the morning I had let him help with getting Jake and Sam dressed while I made up packed lunches for all the children so I hadn't noticed the marks straight away. This, quite rightly, annoyed Phil as part of my role was to check the children and keep them safe, but another part of my role was to observe the relationship between the children and their parents, or children and their adoptive families, once introductions were under way.

Foster carers see so much more than a social worker does when they work so closely with families because the relationship is different and both birth and adoptive families tend to relax more when there are no social workers around. This means that sometimes unguarded comments are made by birth family that can result in a child permanently being removed from a family.

This fact was borne out when I had to do a supervised contact for another little family and while I was alone with the birth father he had disclosed to me so much information about his drug dealing, where he got his drugs and who his clients were (which included another little family that would share our lives a few years down the road) because I wasn't a 'fucking social worker' and to this man I was his 'mate', and he knew I wouldn't 'grass him up'. What this person should have realised was that all my loyalties actually lay with his children and all the children that shared our family life so, once I arrived home I spoke at length to the social worker involved with that case and the children ended up living a much more secure and happy life with a fantastic adoptive family a few years down the line.

So, foster carers have a duty at all times while supervising contact between parents and their children to be vigilant and have no option but to be the eyes and ears for the social worker…and it's vital that we observe properly and don't allow our personal feelings to cloud over or alter our 'professional' view in any way .

The problem with me and Howard at that time was that we were seeing direct evidence of how hard Steve was working to get his sons home and had to work hard ourselves not to get too focused on that as well. We had to remain as detached as possible from the emotions that surrounded Steve and the boys and the relationships we were witnessing and remain focused on what would be in the boys' best interest in the long term.

That fine line was constantly there. We could bend a few rules, but some had to remain absolutely rigid.

The problem with Phil was that he was too focused on Jake and Sam returning to their mum and sisters. He didn't appear to see that Jane was struggling with bringing up her two little girls who she clearly adored and to throw into the equation two little boys that she didn't even want to look after would jeopardise her whole family. Without appearing to see the wider picture Phil had decided that Steve couldn't see the boys outside of our home (or at least if outside of our home it had to be with me in tow so to speak) for a couple of weeks.

This put added strain onto our family as it was one thing to have the choice to stay and spend time with someone but another when it was compulsory. We got on well by now with Steve, but I still needed time to do normal things, which I had strict instructions I couldn't do, such as change beds and do housework that meant I wasn't in the same room as the children at all times when Steve was there. It also meant that Steve would have to tag along to the school and shops if he was still visiting his children at times that I had to be somewhere else.

I guess we were fortunate that Steve was as focused on getting his children home as Phil appeared to be at getting them back to their mother, because he turned up daily and didn't complain once about the regime that had now been placed on him. Steve actually appeared relieved that he would now have a witness to let the social services know how he was with his children and, more importantly, how they were with him.

Chapter 19

It was during this period, which was fourteen weeks since Jane had seen Sam and thirteen weeks since she had seen Jake, that I received a telephone call from her. It was quite late at night and she apologised for not phoning earlier, saying she had meant to call three weeks before but had forgotten, then had been too busy. I wondered how anyone could just forget their children were living just around the corner from them but said nothing. I knew better than to judge people's actions because I didn't know what was going on in her life at that time and of course, she may well have been suffering from depression which would have made a difference to the way she thought things through.

So, there was Jane talking to me, saying that Steve was everything horrendously horrible in her life and the boy's lives. Every bit of trouble she was having was down to Steve and the way he was behaving. Jane told me she had been evicted from their home, which had been repossessed by the mortgage company because Steve had stopped paying the mortgage. How was a man supposed to work to pay a mortgage and feed himself when the social worker wanted him to have daily contact to prove that he not only loved his children but was capable of bringing them up? Steve had had no option but to stop working if he wanted his children, but in doing so, he had also created problems because now he had no money to feed and clothe them. What an unbearable no win situation to be in.

Because Jane had lost her home she said, she was now unsure as to where she would be living, though stressed that she had been given an option of one area but she had to keep that a secret because she didn't want Steve to find out. Jane was also quite adamant that she didn't want Phil or any other social worker involved in any aspect of her life and that she wanted him to stop pestering her. Phil was to keep away…just leave her alone as she only wants her children and that included (for now) 'her' boys. Jane felt she didn't want or need a social worker in her life because she could manage quite nicely on her own.

Having said she didn't know where she was going to be living, she then contradicted herself and said she wanted the boys to move in with her now because she had a room all ready for them with a cot and bed in it…all nicely decorated and ready for two little boys to just move in…

Jane said that her boyfriend no longer featured in her plans and that the planned wedding had now been cancelled. Jane said her life was going to be just her and the boys and her daughters…she loves them all and missed her sons so much she just wanted them back now and not when it suited Steve or Phil.

Jane appeared quite animated as she spoke and told me that if she wanted to she could just take the children home with her tomorrow as there was no care order on them, it was all voluntary and no-one could stop her doing whatever she wanted to do. I was quite concerned to hear her talking like that and thought she may well have had a bit to drink or perhaps had smoked something but remained calm and just listened to her.

Jane complained how unfair it was that Steve saw Jake and Sam every day and thought it was time he let her see them as well, she told me I wasn't to let Steve know she wanted to see the children, but then said I'd have to because he saw them every day so he would find out anyway.

Jane didn't appear to understand that she could have seen Jake and Sam every day of the past fourteen weeks if she had wanted to. Phil would have been very keen on accommodating this and, though it would have been reluctantly done, I knew Steve would have agreed to see the boys for half days instead of full days so they could spend time with their mum.

We had a long chat and Jane, jumping from subject to subject while talking didn't seem at all surprised when I told her in response to a question, that they didn't ask after her or their sisters. As she appeared to be bouncing all over the place and very emotional at times, I did my best to keep her calm because the last thing I wanted was for her to arrive at our home that late at night and cause a scene which would no doubt disturb not only our family but our neighbour's families as well. I explained to her that I would have to speak with Phil about her wish to see the children if she wasn't going to, as he was in charge of the case at that time. Jane agreed to this but said 'Just keep him away from me'.

After about an hour of talking and trying to calm her down, Jane suddenly said she had to go and put the phone down. Jane was right in her thinking that Steve couldn't stop her turning up and just taking Jake and Sam from our home, but she was wrong if she thought Phil couldn't stop her. I certainly knew Phil wouldn't let her take the children out before he had evidence of her new address. It would be interesting to know what he would do following my telephone call to him in the morning.

The following morning, once Claire and James had been dropped off to school I went straight home to telephone Phil and recount the telephone conversation from the previous night.

Phil sat listening quietly while I chatted. He had barely mentioned Jane or her situation to me for some weeks now, appearing to be focusing all his attention on how Steve was coping and pressing me to be very vigilant when he was with Jake and Sam.

There was silence at the other end of the line and then a sigh. When Phil started to talk I could almost see him smiling. Phil was in my opinion, a ladies man, but he was also very much a man who didn't like to be told what he could and couldn't do. He told me that he would be speaking to Jane at some point in the future, but that it wouldn't be that day. If she didn't want to speak with him that was fine for now. However, would I make it very clear to her that she could only see Jake and Sam at 10.00am on the Friday of that week (it was now Tuesday) for two hours, which would be supervised by me and would take place in our home. She could not arrive early and she was to leave at midday at the latest and not a minute after. I was to make it clear that if she was late arriving she lost that time. If she tried to see the children or remove them from our home before or during this contact there would be an EPO (Emergency Protection Order) placed on them and social services would then implement full care proceedings.

I was pleasantly surprised by Phil's attitude and apparent about turn in his approach to Jane. Perhaps he was starting to feel that Steve just may have something in him and about him that would provide a more decent and stable life for his children than their mother could.

Shortly after I had been speaking with Steve Jane telephoned me. She complained that she had been trying to call me for over twenty minutes and certainly sounded angry. I explained to her that I had been talking to Phil regarding the phone call the previous evening and told her what he had said.

Jane appeared to become even more annoyed and shouted that she didn't want to take the boys away, she just wanted to see them and couldn't understand why everyone was trying to stop her. She didn't seem able to comprehend that having absolutely no contact for the previous fourteen weeks would go against her. She shouted that it was wrong that Steve could see 'her' children at any time he chose to, which was every day, while she had to book an appointment! Also, as far as she was concerned, it was wrong that Steve could see them without supervision and take them out but she couldn't. She wouldn't accept that Steve had been consistent in his daily visits and commitment to seeing Jake and Sam while she had chosen to stay away, and clearly she wasn't aware that Steve was, for now, only seeing the children with me being around. I didn't enlighten her to this fact though as I clearly felt if she wanted information about the boys she should speak to Phil.

This angry telephone call ended with Jane telling me she would let me know if she would visit on Friday later in the week…and told me to just make sure Phil knew to keep away from her as her life was nothing to do with him.

Jane didn't telephone again during the week and failed to turn up on the Friday, which was a shame, as though I hadn't told Jake and Sam that she was coming to see them I'd had to cancel Steve's visit for that day. Having discussed with Phil Jane's anger during the telephone call on the Tuesday, it was considered the best option to keep them apart. Had Jane arrived and upset the children, it would not have been fair for Steve to have to deal with two emotional little boys while he was still feeling quite vulnerable himself.

It appeared Phil was also now having a change of heart regarding Steve and was giving a little helping hand to him, albeit a very little helping hand. He had also supported Steve's application to the court for a residency order, which would mean he could have his children living with him if he was successful.

Phil had told me that he was divorced and remarried. He said that when he was first divorced he'd had nowhere to live, no money and was sleeping on a beach some nights, but he had managed to pick himself up and get himself sorted out and that was what he wanted Steve to do. 'It's not impossible' was Phil's attitude to what he expected of Steve and he seemed to put obstacles in the way all the time to test Steve's commitment and resolve.

Chapter 20

It was four weeks before Jane telephoned again. During those four weeks Steve had been visiting the children on a daily basis and had started taking them out on his own again. Everyone benefitted from this as Jake and Sam (as young as Sam was) seemed more relaxed being able to lead a near normal life, coming and going as they wished. Visits to the park were more frequent as Steve had the time to do these things while I had the baby and older children to care for and a home to run.

I had also found out during those four weeks that when Jane had telephoned me late in the evening that she had done so from John's home. Poor John, not only a neighbour but a friend as well, had told me that she had arrived quite drunk and alone in the early part of the evening, saying she needed someone to talk to. Having not had anything to do with Jane for some months, John had felt sorry for her and let her into his home. Apparently she had asked to use his telephone and once we had finished talking she had fallen asleep on the settee. When John had tried to get her to her feet she had just flopped onto the floor and he had finally managed to get her out of his home at three-o-clock in the morning...then he discovered she had taken some money that he'd left on his coffee table. He was certainly not going to let her into his home again.

But I digress…Jane telephoned at lunchtime while I was alone as Steve had already collected the children and taken them off to the park for the day. Jane sounded very depressed and told me that all her problems were still down to Steve. She insisted that she loved and missed her children and knows she gets drunk too often, but that was the only way she knew how to cope with everything that was going on in her life at the moment.

She complained that Steve was a drinking man and wouldn't change so Jake and Sam wouldn't be properly looked after by him. Jane went on to say she had settled into her new home and the girls liked their new school. I thought Jane had possibly already had a drink as she bounced from one topic to another because the next thing she was saying was that she had become pregnant, married, had her children and loved them all and looked after them the best she could. If that wasn't good enough then it was tough because she was having the boys back.

She remained adamant that she would not speak with Phil regarding seeing Jake and Sam. Even when I explained she would need to speak to Phil to discuss the children's future she said she wouldn't do that. Jane ended the call after saying that Steve would stop her seeing her children if he could, though she had chosen herself not to see them for some months now, and said that Steve blamed a lot of her problems on 'that bloke I met', followed by 'Steve's macho self couldn't cope with it'.

I wondered how many men, macho or not, could cope with their wife/partner meeting a new man and starting a relationship with them. The last thing Jane said as she rung off was that she was going to meet a friend for lunch, and then she was gone. I didn't know where she was now living and had no telephone number for her though I had tried to get one. I knew Phil had no way of contacting her either so she had actually, without realizing it, written herself out of any plans for the children's future.

Chapter 21

During all this time the plans for Nathan's future had been slowly progressing. Nathan was an absolutely adorable baby with a gorgeous little smile for everyone. He was now six weeks old and his age assessment had gone well. Happily he responded to everything that was going on around him and had even started to smile and reach his little hand out, though he wasn't quite grasping the toys that were placed near him, which wasn't really a problem because he was at least responding to them being there.

We had an appointment arranged to meet with his birth parent's solicitor as they were desperate to have him returned to them, though everyone knew that this just wasn't going to happen.

The meeting was a very sad one.

I think everyone involved with this family felt so very sad for Nathan's parents. It wasn't their fault they had mental health issues that were too huge to overcome and no amount of support from social services would ever be enough to ensure this baby had a happy and secure childhood with them.

This was the last meeting I had with the solicitor, having met him when I first learned of the case at the hospital and ended with him taking a very clear message back to the parents that there would be no parenting assessment. There would also be no contact visits, which also meant they would have no final goodbye contact.

A final contact was something I hadn't even considered would not happen. All of the families I had worked with had been offered a final visit, but it was felt that it would be too painful for Nathan's parents to cope with and too risky a situation to place a baby and social workers in as the parents may become so distressed that they became violent.

The relief I felt in knowing that Nathan was safe now and his future was already sorted if they could find that very special family for him, was tinged with a sadness for his birth parents because they were not abusive and neglectful people, they were ill. Unfortunately, just too ill to be able to give a child what they need to grow and develop to their full potential.

While life was carrying on with my family, Steve and his family and of course Nathan, I hadn't realised how tired I was starting to feel.

I expected to feel tired but now it was almost excessive tiredness…this had started before Jenny and Chloe had moved on to the therapeutic unit and I had put it down to the extreme amount of time I'd had to be awake and alert in order to keep our children safe as well as Jenny and Chloe safe…I didn't have those same issues in my life now.

Though we were very busy with five children and a new baby to care for (as well as taking time to care for each other), Howard and I were now having relaxed evenings and the weekends were a pleasure because we had plenty of time to spend just with our home grown children and Nathan because Steve now took Jake and Sam out for a least a part of every day.

Steve had finally moved out of his car and into a flat with a friend of his. It was somewhere close to us and I knew, this time he was telling the truth. So many times in the past months he had told everyone he was sharing a flat when in fact he had spent the coldest part of the year living out of his car with its broken window and chill winds all around him. Now I knew exactly where his flat was and at times he had waved to me from the window as I passed. He had also continued working fixed part-time hours in a local bar so had some money in his pocket.

Life was moving on and things were starting to look up for Steve at last.

Howard convinced me it was now time to give myself some consideration and pop in to see the doctor. We didn't realise when I made that appointment that I was just eight weeks away from a hospital stay and major surgery…but such is life, and at the same time, if you look at the positives, we were only sixteen weeks away from life starting to get back to normality…well, our kind of normality at least.

Chapter 22

The summer came and went in a haze of activities. The school holidays were suddenly upon us and I had six children all day, every day, with the exception that Steve took his children out for a few hours each day, although some of those days our children chose to join them and we would all enjoy a picnic in the park.

Our children were growing and Edward and James would spend time at their friend's homes, though more often than not their friends would also be in our home along with Claire's friends, so instead of six children quite often there were more than ten. In addition, James had decided he wanted to learn to cook and in order to make sure what he was cooking tasted good he tested it out on his friends. This meant that most days from about 11.00am there would be a steady stream of children knocking on the door, asking to play with Edward or James. Word had quickly spread around the neighbourhood that our James was quite a good little cook and all would be welcome in our home!

As much as I loved children, I was relieved when it was time for us to go on our holidays with just our own family and the baby. Jake and Sam were going to be spending the two weeks we were away with Steve at his parent's home. They were very excited about spending more time with their grandparents. We were just happy that Steve's parents appeared to be supporting him in his efforts to get his children home at last.

This was to be the longest time Jake and Sam would have spent as a solid block with their dad since they joined our family and Phil wanted to see how he coped.

By choice, I think Phil would have preferred it if Steve had looked after the boys on his own without the support of his parents, because he was treating their holiday as some sort of assessment while waiting to see if Steve was successful in his application to the court for the residency order, but the reality was that even if Steve was taking his children home on a permanent basis, he would have his parent's support wherever he was living because they had finally come to realise that he was committed to them and they were committed to him, or so I thought as we packed up all the bags and loaded the cars with children and baggage and set off on our holidays, having waved Steve, Jake and Sam off on theirs.

Two weeks is just never long enough to get in a whole year's worth of relaxing and recuperating. We returned home after the fortnight had whizzed past with excited but tired children, all nicely tanned and full of tales to tell their friends of the adventures they had been on while we were away. Howard and I were also relaxed and tanned, though we of course had two weeks of laundry to plough through and two weeks of gardening to catch up on.

Then Steve arrived with Jake and Sam looking tired and totally worn out.

Steve looked so down and miserable and complained that Jake and Sam were quite a handful. He said that he couldn't have them for the following day as it was just too much and wasn't convenient.

What a lot can change in just two weeks. I wondered what had happened while they had all been spending what should have been a fun time at Steve's parents' home to have caused such a change in him.

Steve phoned later that evening and said he had decided he would have the children the following day for a couple of hours, but chose not to join us for a meal in the evening which was unusual as he normally always accepted an invitation because it gave him more time with Jake and Sam as well as some adult conversation.

While Steve and the children had been out I'd had a call from Phil who informed me that Steve had been successful in getting his residency order for Jake and Sam.

I was ecstatic for him and expected him to be full of news about this and what they had done while they were away on holiday, but when they got home he just appeared to be so very flat.

Perhaps, I thought, this is how the realization of the enormity of bringing two energetic little boys up hits you. Sadly it seemed this wonderful news, something he had worked so hard for, didn't appear to make him a very happy man.

I noticed a bruise on Sam's bottom when I changed him after Steve had left that day and two days later another one appeared on his outer thigh. I knew I would have to speak to Phil about this, but was starting to feel the tiredness creeping in and there was this constant pain in my stomach that just wouldn't go away and I felt, I just felt so bloody irritable most of the time and in no mood to speak to a social worker who would just tell me he had told me so. He knew Steve was no good all along and this would just prove how right he had been.

I decided to leave it a day or two before making that phone call. No good talking to Phil while I felt like I did, but encouraged Steve to see the children in our home for a few days so I could see how things were going for him and the boys. This was not too hard to do as Steve seemed to be quite down himself and in need of adult company. I figured that if Steve was seeing the children in our home I could once again observe the relationship between father and sons and maybe he would relax enough to say whatever it was that was bothering him. We also needed to start planning for if, and when, the children would be going to live with him now he had the residency order. I also had to prepare him for the possibility of helping more with the children. I now knew there was a very real possibility of me going into hospital in the near future as I had an appointment to see my consultant the following week and was also aware that he would tell me surgery was necessary sooner, rather than later.

It was now over nine months since Steve and his family had entered our lives. In all that time we hadn't had a cross word between us. We were aware when Steve was annoyed with someone or a situation aggravated him and we knew when he was sad and upset, but these emotions didn't affect the relationship we had worked so hard at building with him. Our relationship was one not only of support for him and his children, but also of teaching him skills he would need to be a full time parent. We had done everything in our power to show Steve he was heading in the right direction and that the fight he was fighting was one well worth it. He knew he had our support and that we would stand up for him and yet here we were, nine months down the road and about to have the worst weekend of the year thrown at us by someone we had grown to like, yet at the same time it was a person totally unknown to us…a side of Steve that we didn't recognise at all.

Chapter 23

Steve came to collect Jake and Sam at 11.00am on the Friday morning. While he had a cup of tea with me I asked him if he could keep the boys until their bedtime as I had some very important errands I had to run and offered to give him food to cook for their dinner. Steve refused to take the food and told me that he would not look after them until their bedtime but would return them *to their home* in time for them to eat their tea with us. I was quite taken aback at his attitude more than his words and pointed out that since the holidays and him getting his residency order he had actually been having the children for shorter periods of time, when, in all honesty, he should actively have been working towards longer periods of .being responsible for his sons, with the children, eventually moving into his home. Steve just became so angry and told me that I was incapable of looking after his children and that I didn't want them or him in my life anyway.

I was so shocked at this outburst and retaliated that Howard and I had helped him out more than we should have. We had supported him over and above what had been expected of us and it would be a good idea if he just took the boys for the day and return them when he was in a better frame of mind, because if my lovely placid Howard had heard how he had spoken to me I think he would have said no more extra help and no more joining our family for meals or spending a couple of hours sharing our company once the children were in bed.

I really just wanted to get to the bottom of where this hostility came from. I thought I knew because sometimes, no matter how much you may want something, the reality of getting it is just too scary and I thought that perhaps, just perhaps, Steve was now very scared of what the future held for him and his boys.

Steve picked Sam up and took Jake by the hand as he left our home, saying he would be back by 4.00pm

A peaceful day ensued and finally it got around to 4.00pm. There was no sign of Steve and the children. I'd had to completely rearrange my day because he was bringing the children home early and now he was late.

I telephoned his sister and asked if Steve and the boys were there. Sharon silently handed the telephone to Steve. I asked him what time he would be coming home with Jake and Sam as I had now been waiting for over half an hour, and he had been the one to choose when to return the children. Steve started to moan about life in general so I asked him to just make up his mind about what he wanted to do regarding the rest of the day. He responded that I demanded too much of him said he couldn't afford to feed his children. I felt like I didn't know the man I was talking to. This wasn't the man who had fought to be allowed to keep his children, the man who had given up his job and social life to keep his children, the man who had stood up to his parents and sister to keep his children. Where on earth had the real Steve gone? Or was this the real Steve?

Suddenly Steve wasn't on the other end of the telephone, it was Sharon screaming at me, 'Why don't you give him some of your money? You get paid to feed them kids so give him some of the fucking money!' I was absolutely shocked Sharon had become so nasty and abusive that when she started swearing at me I replaced the receiver and walked away.

Yes, she was right that I did got paid towards the cost of feeding the children that shared our home. I also had money towards their clothes and every aspect of their care. The allowances foster carers got back then though were nowhere near what it costs to cover all expenses that are incurred, and certainly didn't include any element of finance to cover feeding their dad all the meals he'd had with us. And the reality, as most people who foster know, is that you subsidised every placement you had because social services just didn't pay enough money for children travelling through the care system.

An hour later the telephone rang and I answered it. By now I had calmed myself down a bit as I really didn't want to be so angry that I'd say something I may later regret. Howard hadn't arrived home yet and our children were all involved with either playing or homework so weren't listening to my end of the conversation. I didn't want them telling their dad that anyone had upset me, especially not someone he had put himself out to support as well.

It was Sharon again, but this time she was speaking very calmly to me and asked me what was going on. I didn't have a clue what was going on. Steve had changed from the lovely kind man that we had known into a stranger, who I didn't like very much.

I explained my position again and reiterated that I had offered Steve food for him and the children, at which point she started getting abusive and screaming down the phone again that I was apparently showing my true colours now and was apparently the nastiest sort of foster parent anyone could ever wish to meet.

Sharon also threatened that she would make sure we never fostered again. Something she could do because she had loads of 'dirt' on me and 'plenty of money to sort you out good and proper!' At this point I calmly told her I was well known to social services for to providing a very good service to the children who shared our home as well as their families. I also pointed out that it would be good to remember that she and her family were also well known for a different reason. That comment was like putting a match to a fuse wire…though not as much as my next comment to her was…

Sometimes events are just too much to be bothered with and as she ranted on I just felt I'd had enough, at least I'd had enough of her and her verbal abuse towards me so simply said 'Oh, piss off you old tart'. I shouldn't have said what I was thinking but the words just slipped out. Once spoken it was too late to take them back. Sharon screeched at me 'I'll fucking sort you out!' and slammed the receiver down. Peace at last - for now.

When Howard arrived home I had to let him know what had happened and the things that had been said. He was as bewildered as I was and suggested we didn't invite Steve in this evening as was normal, but instead ask him to say his goodnights to the children at the front door.

Steve arrived home a couple of hours later. As Howard requested, he wasn't invited into our home to help settle the children to sleep and enjoy a cup of coffee with us. Instead he said goodbye to the children on the doorstep and left. Such a sad end to the day and I hoped we would soon be back to how it had been between us. I had to explain in as simple language as possible to Jake and Sam that I was going to be very busy for the next few days so they would have to be ready to go when daddy arrived and say goodbye to daddy in the car.

We had quite an awful weekend with Steve calling to collect the children and driving off looking so miserable and then saying nothing when he dropped the boys' home again. Jake and Sam picked up on the tensions and played up a bit when they were at home so I wondered what sort of time they were giving Steve when they were out, but at least there were no fresh bruises or marks on their little bodies, which is possibly why I totally forgot to mention any concerns I'd had a few days earlier, well, that and the fact that I was still somewhat in shock myself at the outburst from Sharon and the new side of Steve that had been presented to us.

Chapter 24

One of the things we still hadn't told Phil was that Steve had often joined us for a meal both during the week and on the odd Sunday. It had started when he had been staying with his sister or friend at the beginning of the placement. He had said he often felt in the way when he was there so the more he could be out of their homes the better.

At that time, I had stopped getting calls from Sharon saying the children should be adopted because her brother couldn't cope which was good. However, she didn't appear to be offering Steve anything more than a bed for the night which was a bit of a let-down, especially as she lived in an affluent area some miles from us in a five bedroom house with only two children. Selfishly I felt she could have offered to have Jake and Sam stay for the weekend now and again but this never happened. Also, as Steve wasn't working then and was officially of no fixed abode because Sharon had refused to let him give her address as where he lived, he had no money coming in to afford much more than his petrol and of course his cigarettes, so I was providing all meals for him and the children on a daily basis, picnics when they went out and a cooked meal when they stayed in. I didn't mind doing this because at least I knew the children were getting a balanced diet, but felt Sharon could have offered some assistance to make it easier for Steve. When Phil had found out about me providing making a picnic for Steve and the boys he had been very angry and told me I was no longer allowed to do that. He said if Steve wanted his kids …he had better start providing for them!

No amount of debate would change Phil's mind on the picnic issue so I sure as hell wasn't going to let him know about the family meals.

The day after Phil had told me I wasn't to make a picnic up Steve arrived to take Jake and Sam out. As he came in the front door I told him I couldn't make him a picnic anymore. He just said that was okay, he'd manage somehow. I remember laughing and telling him that all I had been told was that I couldn't make a picnic, but not that I wasn't allowed to provide the food for one! I told Steve to go make his own hamper up from the food in the kitchen. I reminded Steve about that time when he came to collect the children the next day because although Steve, me and Howard were more friendly now, the ice still needed to be melted. This seemed to do the trick nicely as Steve laughed and walked into the kitchen, thanking me for all the help and support we have given him since the boys arrived.

When Steve returned that afternoon we sat and talked while Jake and Sam played with their toys.

And finally told me that the holiday had not been what he had hoped for. He said that his parents had started at him almost as soon as he walked through the door about having Jake and Sam adopted. He said they just went on and on about how much better the children would be without him and how much better he would be without them. Because of the constant 'ear bashing' he'd had from his parents he felt that Jake had picked up that something was wrong and had then started being naughty. Once Jake started playing up Sam started to become sullen and tearful. Steve said he'd had the two weeks from hell and was just so glad when we got home from our holiday and he could just drop the children back to us and walk away for a few hours.

Steve went on to say that while he was at his parents and they were talking at him all the time about getting Jake and Sam adopted, his sister would also telephone and he'd be getting told the same by her. The children were so moody and naughty all the time that he just knew he would never be able to look after them on his own. Then, when he had dropped the children off and gone to see his sister, she had started at him all over again, telling him how he would have no life with two kids tied to his ankles.

He apologised for the telephone call when his sister was so rude to me, shrugged his shoulders and asked 'How will I manage without you and Howard to believe in me? What will I do when we all leave your home for the last time?' He added that he was so afraid of getting it all wrong, that he just didn't know what to do for the best.

I was absolutely appalled. How could a mum and dad treat their son so badly and dismiss their grandchildren so casually while they were all supposed to be having a lovely holiday together? How nasty could a sister be who had everything from fur coats and jewellery, a lovely home, nice car as well as two lovely children and a husband to pay for it all. How could she think it normal for a man to just walk away from his children? I wondered if she would have been able to walk away from her own.

The following day Steve arrived and told me Sharon said she would have nothing more to do with him. I was stunned because initially, though she made it clear she wanted Jake and Sam to be adopted, she had at least seemed to be supportive of her brother and nephews in recent months. In hindsight, I guess I'd thought she was being supportive because she had been quiet.

I wondered if this was her way of forcing the issue regarding adoption. If Steve had no family support the social services would have to follow the plan to have Jake and Sam adopted. She wouldn't look like the 'bad guy' because it would be social services making the decision without her being involved.

Fortunately for Steve, and unknown to Sharon and Steve's parents, around this time Phil also seemed to be having a change of heart. He had started the ball rolling about getting Steve a council house, and though this would take some time to get organized, at least we were all finally travelling in the same direction at the same time.

With Sharon now out of the picture, Steve also returned to the nicer person he had been during the earlier phase of our relationship. We once again welcomed him into our home where he spent much more time with the boys.

We hadn't seen nor heard from Jane for months now as she had moved with her daughters to another area. She let Phil know that she had decided she didn't want to be involved with Jake and Sam's childhood on any level, telling him that *he may as well let Steve have them* because at least that way they would be with one parent. Maybe this was why Phil had changed his mind and started to be more helpful with getting things organised so that Steve and the boys could one day have a home of their own.

Now the residence order was in place, Steve decided that he'd have to get a proper part-time job for a short time at least, so he could get some money together to buy whatever he would need once he got a council flat. He managed to get an evening job, which paid enough for him to move from his friend's flat into a furnished flat closer to where we lived. This still allowed him day time visits with the children and the time to join them for some early evening meals. Everything just seemed to be moving along nicely now.

Like all good plans though, life often has a way of changing them...sometimes for better...sometimes for worse. What happened for us was a bit of both.

Following my visit to see the consultant it was decided that I had to go into hospital within a matter of weeks, rather than months. We had both been putting this day off for so long since Jenny and Chloe had moved to the therapeutic unit, which was when I had first started to feel poorly. Because so many children had needed help in quick succession we had delayed doing anything about how I felt but knew that now, after delaying things for the best part of a year, we had to put my health before any other commitments. Howard and I talked things over with Phil and explained that as far as we were concerned Steve had done more than prove himself in his commitment to looking after Jake and Sam.

It was also clear to Phil that Steve had received no help or support from his parents when he had stayed with them for the two weeks we had been away. In fact, if anything, they had actually made his life so much tougher even than when he had been living in his car - at least then, he'd had somewhere to come and warm up and have a friendly chat without getting moaned at or having people try to force their opinions down his throat.

Steve had also, over the time we had been involved with him and the boys, stopped his drinking bouts, learned how to put safe boundaries in place and become the parent that he needed to be, rather than letting Jake act like the parent and make decisions that he was just too young to make.

Phil left our home with a promise to see what he could do to move things along a little quicker. None of us thought it would be in Jake and Sam's best interest to have a respite placement while I was in hospital and with the best will in the world, there was no way Howard could go to work all day then come home and look after our children, a baby and two lively toddlers as well as find time to visit me.

A couple of days later Phil arrived at our home while Steve was there playing with Jake and Sam. His face was grave when he walked in and told Steve he had some news to give him and didn't think it right that it should be done over the phone.

Steve looked from Phil to me. I had no idea what Phil was going to say but presumed it had to be something serious. Maybe Jane had changed her mind and was going to fight Steve for the children?

Phil just stood there looking at us, then smiled and told Steve he had a new home in a village a few miles from us!

Oh my goodness. The look on Steve's face was such a picture. He looked, open-mouthed at Phil, then me, then back to Phil again. There were tears in his eyes as he realised that this was it - He was actually going to be taking his children home with him soon.

True to his word Phil did appear to make mountains move over the following two weeks as he got all the paperwork sorted out which would enable Steve to care for his children.

At last Steve would have an address of his own which meant he could have the financial support he needed to look after Jake and Sam which had been denied him so far.

Phil also made sure that furniture and other household necessities were purchased and in place ready for the big day when this little family would set out on the road to what we all hoped would be a happy future.

The only odd thing that happened at this time, was that Phil refused to allow Steve to tell me and Howard where he would be living with the children. He also refused him any contact with us once the children left our home.

This was unusual because in all the placements we had been involved in until then, once the children had either returned to live with their parents or had moved on via adoption, we had remained for a short time a source of support for the family should they need it, even if this was just by the parents making telephone contact. How strange, we felt, that this would not be in place for Steve and the children.

Steve was told there would be no contact from the day they walked out of our front door, so he had best make sure he was prepared and had said all that would ever need to be said before that day arrived.

The end of Jake and Sam's stay with us was a mixture of happiness, sorrow and very much activity. We only had a week to pack up all their bits and pieces and prepare for them to leave. At the same time I needed to pack all the paraphernalia that would be needed by Elizabeth who was going to look after Nathan for a couple of weeks while I was in hospital.

It was strange for our own children to be saying goodbye to the boys at a time when I would also be leaving our home, which meant that we wouldn't have any special time with only our family at home.

Finally, with hugs for everyone, Steve walked out of our home with his sons. The last thing he said was how sorry he was that he couldn't keep in touch with us.

I'm not sure what Phil said to ensure Steve remained silent...but silent he remained.

Postscript

Nathan:

Following my surgery I returned home after ten days to a quiet house with only Edward, James and Claire to care for...not that I was up to looking after anyone at that time, so it was lucky there were no school holidays on the horizon.

The following week Howard, Edward, James and Claire happily collected Nathan from Elizabeth's and, between Howard and Elizabeth, who came every day with her foster children to look after Nathan for me while Howard was at work, we managed to get through the following three months while I recovered and got my strength back.

Our parents helped out at weekends and took our children to school during the week. They looked after them after-school, dropping them home once Howard had returned home from work.

It was some months after I had fully recovered that Howard and I were introduced to a lovely couple who would go on to adopt Nathan. They seemed to be a very happy couple and very calm in their approach to parenting. They already had a young daughter who was so excited at the thought of having a baby brother that we felt, like the social worker, they were the right family for this very special little boy.

Introductions were done over a two week period and watching this little family as they bonded was lovely. Nathan was a very lucky little lad as, though the parents were made aware of all the potential hazards he could face as he grew up, their quiet, calm manner gave reassurance that it would be unlikely he would have the serious mental health problems his parents did.

It's now over twenty years since we met this family and I'm happy to say that we are still in touch via Christmas cards which we fill with news about what has been happening for our families during the year. As far as we are aware, Nathan has escaped the future he might have had if he hadn't been given the opportunity to live in a calmer, more peaceful and normal environment.

Perhaps 'normal' is the wrong word to use, because what's normal for some is abnormal for others.

Nathans home life with his new family was not haphazard; as it would have been had he remained with his birth parents...

Had he stayed with his birth parents there would have been times periodically that his parents were being hospitalized for their own or others protection. At these times Nathan would probably have had to enter into the care system as a respite placement and with the best will in the world, there are always going to be issues arising with respite placements as no-one usually knows how long they will last.

Respite placements cause so much disruption to children as they are seldom in the children's local area, so they then have to have transport to and from school. After school activities can become disrupted as well as any peer relationships that have been formed. His life would not have been as secure and grounded as it had been because of his adoption.

On a sad note regarding Nathans birth parents, I have been told that his mother never came to terms with losing her second child. She was found dead some years after his adoption while undergoing treatment for mental health issues and depression.

I have no information about his birth father.

Jake and Sam:

It was about nine years after Steve, Jake and Sam left our home that, walking home one day, I saw a man standing outside of some offices having a cigarette. He smiled at me and waved. Although I had no idea who he was, I smiled back and nodded my head. As I got closer to him I thought he looked familiar but still had no idea who he was but thought maybe he was a parent of one of the children that had attended my Beaver Colony a few years earlier…

The man suddenly laughed out loud and said "Hello Lorraine…you don't recognise me do you?" As soon as he opened his mouth, I did and just stared at him.

Steve had aged very well over those few years. He was in a suit and looked well-fed and very happy with his life.

We stood chatting and Steve told me that he had kept his promise to me, avoiding women until both Jake and Sam were both at school, and then waiting until Jake had started senior education. He was now in a relationship with someone he had met through his local church and everything was going well for him and the boys.

I invited Steve to our home, giving him our address as we had moved and told him to come anytime, but I never saw him again. I did, however, receive a lovely surprise one day seven years later.

A friend from our church asked me if we knew a man called Steve who had two sons called Jake and Sam. When I told her we did, she said she worked with him and our name had come up in conversation. He had asked her to say hello to us and asked if he could have our address because he had lost it all those years ago. Shortly after our meeting his job had been relocated to another area by the company he worked for so hadn't been around to see me in passing.

A few weeks later we received a lovely letter from Steve with a photo of him, Jake and Sam, taken on a beach while on holiday abroad. The three of them looked so happy, with Jake and Sam having grown into fine looking young men.

Steve said in his letter that he had struggled at first with being a single parent and having the boys with him twenty four hours a day. However, Phil had actually pulled out all the stops and put a superb support package in place for him, with Jake and Sam both going to the local play school for a few hours every day. He said again, in the letter, that he had kept that promise and was still in a happy relationship with the lady he had told me about, but went on to say he had experienced a few problems when, two years earlier Jake and Sam had asked to meet their birth mother. Steve had managed to find where she was living but she didn't want anything to do with them. They had managed to form a fragile relationship with one of their half-sisters which he hoped they would build on and, one day, perhaps their mother would decide she would also work at having a relationship with them.

Steve wrote that due to the second rejection by their mother Sam had turned to drugs. The whole family had endured a rough few months as everything seemed to spiral out of control, but they seemed to be on an even keel again now.

We know with Steve that news of how he and the boys are doing will be sporadic and totally out of the blue, but it is nice to know that for now, all is good in their lives.

Tormented

Fostering? Easy, we would look after children who weren't looked after properly or maybe smacked too hard... No-one prepared us for this nightmare'

The scream, when it came, was unlike anything I had ever heard before. It was so piercing it made every hair on my body stand on end, and the memory of the terror I felt then, in that instant, has never gone away. I flew out of my bed and ran into the girls' room, convinced that something truly, utterly devastating was happening to one of the children. It was.

Comments about Tormented

"A significant book because of the insight it brings to the reader of the complexity of relationships, and trauma for the cared for and the carer with fostering children. This book entertains, educates and arouses all sorts of emotions for the reader. It is also an inspirational book as it sends out messages of hope that there are some people who care a lot about others and have the patience and courage to support and offer a decent framework for those who need it."

"Tormented is presented in business-like but graphic detail and there is no doubt as to the validity of the story contained therein. Painful experiences are vividly described and the difficulties encountered in attempting to analyse the behaviour and thought processes of foster children, influenced as they are by previous 'care and attention', are identified. This work is competent and knowledgeable and is virtually an informal treatise.

Chapter 1

I'd had the phone call on Tuesday, enquiring when the boys we were fostering were leaving. Having told the social worker they were due to return to their family on the following Monday, I'd been asked to consider looking after two little girls.

I told the social worker that, in theory, we would have them. Now I would need to discuss the placement with my husband, and weigh up the implications on our own children, as our six year old daughter Claire was used to being the only 'little lady' in our home. Though our children always welcomed each new 'brother' or 'sister' with open arms, foster parents have to think about the possibility of disrupted nights and the open aggression that some children bring with them.

Jealousies can also arouse from either our children or our fostered children and of course, the change in routine that happens with each new placement. Consideration has also to be given to such things as fitting in our childrens' after school activities and supporting children who have contact in or away from our home.

We also had to speak with our eldest son David, who was settled at university but still came home for the odd weekend when he wasn't busy studying, or carrying out one of the many pursuits he had taken up over the past year.

There was also the added concern that due to Jennys' age she would attend the same school as Claire. This had caused a small issue with a previous placement, though Claire and Vikki, being the same age had been in the same class which had meant Claire had no time away from her. At least with the age difference Claire would get lesson time away from Jenny.

Julia, the social worker explained that the children had been bought to England from Wales, where they had been living with their grandparents, but couldn't return there, now having given me as much information as she could, we ended the phone call.

Monday morning arrived quickly, our youngest sons Edward and James as well as Claire had been taken to school and I was busy packing the last few bits of clothes and toys ready for the social worker to take the boys home to their parents.

It had been lovely having them in our home, but it was always much nicer to have a happy ending to a placement; however that was reached, return or adoption was better than long term care.

Once the boys had left I got on with changing the beds and sorting out wardrobe space for the girls.

I also climbed into the loft to sort out a special 'cuddle' to leave on the girls' bed.

I made sure to always keep a large supply of soft cuddly toys up there as experience had taught us the children we cared for seldom arrived with anything to comfort them once they had gone to bed and we knew, irrespective of the childrens' age, a soft toy was usually hugged tightly if only while the children were settling in to their new home and the older children, only if they thought we couldn't see them.

Once that was done I set about tidying up the playroom, making sure I left out some toys for the girls.

Howard and I had discussed the issues that Julia had told me about.

On the surface there seemed little to concern us.

Having been asked if we would facilitate contact at our home, we felt fairly confident that this was going to be an 'okay' family, one which we would form a relationship with and at some time in the future, start working towards the girls returning home to either their mother or extended family members.

Once we had decided this was a placement we could work with, we had asked the children if they would like two little girls to stay.

Obviously, being bound by the constraints of confidentiality and our childrens' ages we didn't tell them about any of the issues, though pointed out that it would mean Claire would be sharing her bedroom with two little girls and it was more likely that they would want to play with her toys and spend time with her.

We always explained to our children that sharing a room meant that they may have disturbed nights, the child may mess their things up or break their toys. They may also steal from them and many had night terrors and wet the bed. Basic information, but important as the last thing we wanted was for any child to have more moves than necessary within the care system, as each move was, to the children we cared for, a rejection.

Once our family had committed to a placement, we stayed committed.

Our children knew that and as young as they were, without realising it, supported Howard and I in the work we chose to do.

Julia arrived with the girls just after 2pm. Even though it was the first time we had met, we had spoken so often on the telephone during the past week about the girls; I felt I knew her well already.

Julia was a bit taller than me, quite slim and blond. She had a relaxed air about her and a ready smile that reached her eyes. The best thing was, she made me feel like she was talking to an equal, something so many social workers didn't quite manage.

Since we had started fostering, so many social workers we'd worked with had spoken to us as though we were one up from the client whose child we were caring for. This was a common complaint from many of the foster carers we had met at the monthly support group I attended at the time.

The girls had been in care for just over a week, staying in what is termed as an 'emergency placement'.

As a rule I don't like having children from emergency placements. This is my own prejudice I know, but it's because it means another move for the children, another 'felt' rejection.

Another down side to taking emergency placements meant that, if the child had been placed for a few weeks, their previous carer had probably been given the clothing allowance, though many didn't send the items purchased for the children with them when they moved on, which could mean quite a considerable financial outlay for my husband as we felt it was important that the children feel part of our family, not only by being included in whatever we were doing, but by looking as though they belonged as well.

Not that our children were ever togged out in designer gear, but they always had nice clothes and looked presentable.

Irrespective of your own personality, society does notice clothes and we had found that a child that dresses similar to their peers is more likely to be accepted by them, especially if joining a classroom where friendships have already been formed.

Commitment is paramount in making a child feel valued and I feel very strongly that should start from day one.

Howard and I also provided emergency cover for the department, which happens when a child suddenly needs to be found somewhere safe to stay without prior planning or warning, but, in general, these children then stayed until their future was sorted out.

The downside to providing emergency placements is that the children come home, or wake in the morning, to an enlarged family with no warning and absolutely no knowledge about age, sex or minor problems they may have to cope with.

Fortunately most of our placements were planned and the emergency ones worked out well, thanks to us knowing our childrens' expectations of their parents and, in the case of daytime emergencies, me knowing how relaxed and accepting Howard was of any decision I made regarding sharing our life and home.

Jenny, aged 5, and Chloe, aged 3 came running up the drive showing no outward concerns about moving into our home.

Even though we had not been foster parents for many years, we were concerned this was a clear indication of an 'attachment disorder'; one more issue we would have to work with as we helped these children come to terms with their past and move on to a better future.

Attachment is a very complex area and can manifest in many different ways. Some children can't even refer to their siblings by their names, preferring to simply say "My brother or my sister", some will sit on the sidelines of life, watching but not participating in activities that they may well enjoy, for fear of a positive reaction that they will not understand or be able to cope with.

Many will deliberately sabotage all attempts to form good relationships because they 'know' they are not worth anything to anyone, and you are just lying to them anyway, just getting ready to dump them like everyone else has. It's just easier if they never get close to you, then you can't hurt them can you.

A childs' ability to relate to others and build relationships can depend on the quality of their early childhood relationships and the trauma they may have experienced.

Though not all apparent irrational behaviours and reactions can be attributed to attachment disorder, it's a good area to look at. It's a good base to begin forming a bond with the child and help them experience the joy of positive attention and praise for good behaviour, rather than avoiding it, though this does need patience as it can take a long time.

As I watched the children coming towards me my initial thoughts, apart from concern at their friendliness, was how pretty they were.

Both had lovely dark hair and pretty blue eyes. They appeared to be dressed nicely and were clean, another plus as most of the children we cared for needed a nice warm bath and change of clothes almost on arrival, not that you could do that as it could be seen as a form of rejection in their eyes, of all that is familiar to them.

No, usually when a child arrived we let them play, explore our home and settle in before having a meal, bath and bedtime story.

Day two was always the start of getting to know them and settling into a routine which would allow for any changes that would evolve slowly as our relationship and hopefully, the child's trust in us grew.

Once the children and Julia were in our home I showed the children into the playroom, while Julia and I sat in the lounge which was the adjoining room, discussing the expectations the department had of us, and ours of them.

Neither Julia nor I were aware as we sat chatting just how harrowing this placement was to become over the following months.

Mia

Ok...

I'm a foster carer who doesn't want this placement.

The department of Social Services know just how to apply pressure...

Oh yes... they get one very good, very friendly, very experienced social worker that I happen to have so much respect for, to make the call, knowing, just knowing that I will possibly surrender and agree to share our home with a child that, to be honest, was the last child in the world that I felt capable of caring for...

Felt capable of feeling anything for...

Felt capable of... anything to do with her.

Hmmmmm, sometimes I'm so bloody shallow you see.

I don't want people to look at me as I go about my business.

I don't want strangers giving me pitying looks or hurrying past pretending they haven't looked in my pram.

I don't want to give up any of the precious time I spend with my birth children and husband.

I want my life to stay just as it is.

Happy and contented.

Oh the lessons I was about to learn.

Comments about Mia

This is a story of love and devotion by foster parents who really do care.

I read your first book with great interest some time ago and was left with a feeling of guilt. The guilt part was to realise how difficult a foster parent's job was on an everyday occurrence. This is something that doesn't come to mind for a normal family...it just isn't thought of by the majority of people.

The story of Mia and your efforts to improve her tiny life is very moving. I felt the reward in your eyes as she opened her little hands to signify her relaxed state, the nurses also witnessing the act.

Chapter 1

"The answers no"

"Please Lizzie, think again..."

"Look Sarah," I said, "I've had this same discussion for the past week with team leaders; link workers; social workers...they all got the same answer. Now they get you to phone and add pressure to me. It's just not fair. I don't feel capable of doing this."

"And what's more...it's got to be written somewhere on our profile the sort of children we will take in"

We were not fussy foster carers, we just knew our comfort zone and liked to stay in it, though this wasn't always easy because sometimes; most times; we started off in our comfort zone then events somehow took us spiralling out of it.

We did not however, like to start outside of it and then spiral further away from what we knew we could do. Oh no; that could be disastrous for everyone involved, especially the child or children that had been placed with us.

"You can't just expect us to say yes all the time...sometimes you are just going to have to accept the no word...like now."

I don't care what you say...go down on your knees...the answer will not be any different for you even if I do like and respect you.

Sarah had listened patiently to me as I rattled on about the unfairness of social workers putting pressure onto foster carers; about how we push ourselves to the limit...do our best...and still they want more.

When we had started fostering years ago we were allowed to say no to all kinds of placements; no boys or perhaps you didn't want girls; no black children or you could turn away white children; no Catholics; Protestants; Jews; no disabilities...no; no; no.

You could be so picky it was untrue.

And, at the risk of getting a slapped wrist...

It was fair.

How cruel is it to place a child with a family that really don't want them to be there, because they are the wrong colour or religion?

That must be torture for the child...to be removed from a birth family that is dysfunctional, only to be placed with a fostering family that will just about 'tolerate' you

That type of foster family is as dysfunctional on another level as the birth family.

No; it is definitely much better to have some choice thrown into the equation.

All we had said no to was a child with disabilities.

By disability we meant major issues with mobility or severe mental disability. I didn't feel it was fair on our young family to take on a child that could be so demanding of our time, making normal days out became too difficult to manage; a child that would actually change our normality into something altogether different; though of course I knew many people did manage and manage very well.

We were happy to work with children who had the smaller disabilities like poor hearing or poor sight, even minor learning disabilities would be manageable, I just knew I couldn't cope with anything major and Howard had to go to work so it would always be me doing most of the child care.

Know your capabilities I thought. Know your limitations.

Not of course that anyone starting out on the rocky road of fostering can possibly know their capabilities.

They may think they do but, it's a funny road to travel as you come up to so many sign posts along the way.

None of them point to the easy route.

Now Howard and I had been happy to care for any child when we first started our fostering career.

Well...so long as they had two arms; two legs; a mouth that worked; and ears that heard.

Being quite naive we figured that just about covered everyone.

And anyway...even post training, initially we still thought we were only going to be looking after kids who had been hit too hard or not fed properly...

Had we known then what we learned as we travelled, maybe we should have said no children who have been sexually abused; under fed; over fed; no child who has had the shite beat out of him; hot baths; cold baths; no child who had druggies for parents...or alcoholics...

And yes, to the child who has disabilities...yes to a child whose diagnosis was non-accidental head injury, hypoxic brain injury, bilateral subdural collections, and haemorrhage, resulting in a child who wasn't showing consistent visual responses, to a child who had physical and mobility problems and was epileptic ...who was under the care of a variety of health professionals that would continue for the foreseeable future and probably into adulthood.

But I digress; we started our fostering career like so many other's...

Blissfully unaware of exactly what we were getting our family into.

Okay...I'll settle for vocation because I suppose that was what it was.

Now it's a career where you can earn big money if you work for the right agency and, from what I've seen from some of the 'carers' I've met over the years, you don't even have to be that good.

Like birth parents...for some reason foster carers standards have to be just 'good enough.'

Whatever 'good enough' means.

For Howard and I, knowing our capabilities and working within that framework, meant taking in who we felt we could care for in the same way we cared for our own children.

We had always given a service to the social services that we would want our children to have if they had ever been in the sad situation of needing to be fostered.

Hell would freeze over before I allowed any of my kids into some of the foster homes I've been in though.

God there are some skanky families out there...but they are nice people you see...

No to be honest I didn't.

I would eventually get so fed up with the 'non judgmental political correctness' of it all.

So what if I judged people.

This was real life.

I don't think there is a person alive that doesn't pass judgement every day on someone...even if it's just to admire a pretty face or complain about a meal.

We are judging.

One social worker told me my standards were too high and that I shouldn't judge everyone by them.

What a laugh.

My standards in my opinion were normal.

1. Clean children...until they went out to play then they were dirty children...no problem because there is always a bath before bedtime and soap before meals.
2. Play with children...this is always more important that getting any housework done as kids grow up...and the housework will still need doing long after I'm dead and buried.
3. Enjoy a childhood...its hard work at times...but fun, and if you are lucky, you can enjoy a childhood all your life.

To save having any hassle from social services regarding the state of our home, I had a cleaner come in twice a week, just because I prefer to play than dust.

Know what you are happy to do, capable of doing and just do the best you can within that remit.

Easy.

Nowadays, in this politically correct world we were supposed to say yes to everyone. This meant even if you did not feel competent to deal with some of the issues that may arise.

"...her foster carer has to go into hospital with another child she is looking after..."

Sarah had started to speak again. I wasn't really listening to what she said.

"...it's only going to be a six week placement. Just respite..."

I'd already spoken with Howard about this baby and we'd both agreed that it wasn't what we wanted to do.

Mia was just too damaged and had too many problems for me to cope with comfortably on a day to day basis on my own.

I knew I couldn't look after her properly. What if I did something wrong and she died?

"...so you see Lizzie, there really is no-one other than you and Howard that I want to care for her."

I laughed and said I was used to social workers trying to get their placements in here and we happily obliged whenever we could; but this is just too much for us to cope with at the moment.

We were very lucky to have such a good reputation, though this often meant that a social worker would phone knowing we were full, but asking when one of our children or group of children would be moving out.

Or maybe we could just squeeze one more little head in.

This also meant we could, to an extent be choosey. If I knew a placement was coming to an end, I also phoned social workers that I liked working with (though there weren't that many of them) to let them know because, as far as I was concerned, if a foster carer and social worker got on, the placement would run smoothly, though not without the problems that the children invariably bought with them.

Rarely did we have any time with just our 'home growns', though our own children never complained as they seemed to like having lots of children to play with as they grew up.

But this...this would be different.

This would be too different, too difficult and too much responsibility.

This was just not going to happen.

"Please Lizzie; it's only for six weeks. I'm her social worker so you know you can trust me. I'll be there anytime you need me and there is a huge support network already set up with the hospital and outside agencies."

"Besides" she said, "I know you. I trust you to do whatever it takes to help this baby and know you will manage."

Bugger it.

The trouble was Sarah was one of the few social workers I had worked with that I truly liked and trusted to work in a child's best interest.

She always listened to whatever information I had to give and, even if she didn't agree with my viewpoint, she considered it and, if warranted, would change her stance. She also laughed and had a sense of humour, something sadly lacking in many social services offices nowadays...I think because everyone is scared of laughing at a joke that somehow 'offends' one person in the office and then there may be disciplinary action and a good worker can lose their job or be demoted which is so sad.

And, unfortunately; Sarah did know me...

"Aawww...Sarah!"

Sod it...I said one word...just one word that I hadn't intended to...

"Okay"

And the rest is history...

"...so long as it's just six weeks. So long as I can phone you when you are at work and I need to know everything is okay. I don't want any bullshit about how good we are; I just want one hundred percent support from you."

I could almost see the smile swimming down the phone line.

Sarah sighed, "Thank you Lizzie. I'm on the other end of the phone and will call in as often as you want."

With that Sarah ended the phone call as she had to get the arrangements moving along.

Even as Sarah ended the call I knew; really knew, that with the best will in the world...she wouldn't always be at the end of the phone.

I knew she would and did have other case loads that were equally as important as Mia...just not to me and my family.

Still, it was only for six weeks...

Printed in Great Britain
by Amazon